ANCIENT COMMUNITIES UNDER ATTACK: ISIS'S WAR ON RELIGIOUS MINORITIES

HEARING

BEFORE THE

COMMITTEE ON FOREIGN AFFAIRS
HOUSE OF REPRESENTATIVES

ONE HUNDRED FOURTEENTH CONGRESS

FIRST SESSION

MAY 13, 2015

Serial No. 114–49

Printed for the use of the Committee on Foreign Affairs

Available via the World Wide Web: http://www.foreignaffairs.house.gov/ or
http://www.gpo.gov/fdsys/

U.S. GOVERNMENT PUBLISHING OFFICE

94–605PDF   WASHINGTON : 2015

For sale by the Superintendent of Documents, U.S. Government Publishing Office
Internet: bookstore.gpo.gov   Phone: toll free (866) 512–1800; DC area (202) 512–1800
Fax: (202) 512–2104   Mail: Stop IDCC, Washington, DC 20402–0001

COMMITTEE ON FOREIGN AFFAIRS

EDWARD R. ROYCE, California, *Chairman*

CHRISTOPHER H. SMITH, New Jersey
ILEANA ROS-LEHTINEN, Florida
DANA ROHRABACHER, California
STEVE CHABOT, Ohio
JOE WILSON, South Carolina
MICHAEL T. McCAUL, Texas
TED POE, Texas
MATT SALMON, Arizona
DARRELL E. ISSA, California
TOM MARINO, Pennsylvania
JEFF DUNCAN, South Carolina
MO BROOKS, Alabama
PAUL COOK, California
RANDY K. WEBER SR., Texas
SCOTT PERRY, Pennsylvania
RON DeSANTIS, Florida
MARK MEADOWS, North Carolina
TED S. YOHO, Florida
CURT CLAWSON, Florida
SCOTT DesJARLAIS, Tennessee
REID J. RIBBLE, Wisconsin
DAVID A. TROTT, Michigan
LEE M. ZELDIN, New York
TOM EMMER, Minnesota

ELIOT L. ENGEL, New York
BRAD SHERMAN, California
GREGORY W. MEEKS, New York
ALBIO SIRES, New Jersey
GERALD E. CONNOLLY, Virginia
THEODORE E. DEUTCH, Florida
BRIAN HIGGINS, New York
KAREN BASS, California
WILLIAM KEATING, Massachusetts
DAVID CICILLINE, Rhode Island
ALAN GRAYSON, Florida
AMI BERA, California
ALAN S. LOWENTHAL, California
GRACE MENG, New York
LOIS FRANKEL, Florida
TULSI GABBARD, Hawaii
JOAQUIN CASTRO, Texas
ROBIN L. KELLY, Illinois
BRENDAN F. BOYLE, Pennsylvania

AMY PORTER, *Chief of Staff*   THOMAS SHEEHY, *Staff Director*
JASON STEINBAUM, *Democratic Staff Director*

(II)

CONTENTS

ANCIENT COMMUNITIES UNDER ATTACK: ISIS'S WAR ON RELIGIOUS MINORITIES

WEDNESDAY, MAY 13, 2015

House of Representatives,
Committee on Foreign Affairs,
Washington, DC.

The committee met, pursuant to notice, at 10 o'clock a.m., in room 2172 Rayburn House Office Building, Hon. Edward Royce (chairman of the committee) presiding.

Chairman ROYCE. This committee hearing will come to order. Today we focus on the minority communities, the many minority communities that are under brutal attack—some of them on the brink of extermination by ISIS—by ISIS principally in Iraq and Syria but elsewhere as well. And we are joined by individuals who have personally faced this threat and are familiar with the extreme hardship with the grief that displaced minorities face in that troubled region.

ISIS has unleashed a campaign of brutal violence, depraved violence, not only against Shia Muslims and fellow Sunnis who do not share their radical beliefs, but against vulnerable religious and ethnic minorities. And as Ms. Isaac put it simply in her prepared testimony, "We cherish ethnic and religious diversity; ISIS hates it."

Many Americans may not realize that Iraq and Syria are home to dozens of ethnic and religious minorities with ancient cultures with deep roots. These communities—Assyrian and Chaldean Christians, Yezidis, Alawites, and others—are under mortal threat in their ancestral homelands. And the mass execution of men, the enslavement of women and children, and the destruction of religious sites, is part of the ISIS effort to destroy these communities, to destroy all evidence of the preexistence of these communities. In fact, ISIS maintains a special battalion. They call it the "demolition battalion." And that battalion is charged with going after art and going after artifacts, religious and historic sites that it considers heretical or idolatrous, and their job is simply to destroy history.

The situation for some of these groups was precarious even before ISIS. According to some estimates, more than half of Iraq's religious and ethnic minorities have fled the country over the last dozen years.

But what they face today is annihilation by ISIS, and the influx of ISIS extremists has become a plague. The fall of Mosul in June of last year uprooted 2 million souls, 2 million human beings. Members will recall the U.S.-led air strikes and operations by Kurdish forces last August to break the siege at Mount Sinjar where thousands of Yazidi refugee families had been trapped by ISIS.

The physical security and welfare of displaced minorities is an immediate priority. Options for U.S. assistance range from additional material support to friendly forces, all the way to creating safe zones or no-fly zones. And while it is important to weigh the costs of each option, we cannot lose sight of the fact that people are being kidnapped, people are being tortured, women are being raped—and children—and they are being killed every day.

Beyond that we need to focus more on their psychological well-being. Many of those people, especially women and girls, have been subjected to unspeakable traumas. The young men are mostly just slaughtered. And as with any displaced population, as their vulnerability increases so does the threat of human trafficking. What can be done to better protect women and girls at risk of slavery?

Finally, what can and should be done to keep these evacuations from becoming permanent? It would be a tragedy if well-intended resettlement fulfilled the goal of ISIS itself, in other words to drive these believers out. Are there ways to support the reconstruction of local institutions and civil society so that post ISIS—and there must be a post ISIS—these communities can return and thrive in their ancestral homelands?

I will now turn to the ranking member, Mr. Eliot Engel of New York, who has been a true leader on Syria and on the humanitarian and human rights disaster in the region, for his opening comments.

Mr. ENGEL. Thank you very much, Mr. Chairman, and thank you as always for calling this important hearing. And let me also thank our witnesses who are joining us today. We are very appreciative that you are here.

This committee has taken a hard look at the brutal campaign ISIS is raging in Iraq and Syria. We have learned about the broader threat ISIS poses across the Middle East and around the world. We know how dangerous this group is. We have heard how many people have lost their homes and their livelihoods and their lives in the wake of this violence.

And today we will focus on the heartbreaking struggles of Christians, Yazidis and Muslims who have defied the barbaric perversion of Islam espoused by ISIS. We will hear about the dangers that these communities face every day, how ISIS has killed, raped and enslaved those who don't fall in line with their fanaticism, and I hope their stories will remind us and our partners and allies around the world that we must do everything possible to help these people.

We will also hear about the attempt by ISIS to erase the history of these communities. We have all seen videos and reports of ISIS destroying ancient sites and historical artifacts in the territories they control. Now these are not random acts of vandalism. ISIS is deliberately targeting cultural property for two reasons. Firstly, to loot and steal cultural artifacts to fund their violent campaigns; and secondly, to destroy what is left in a calculated effort to eradicate minority cultures.

This form of psychological warfare against the Yazidis, Christians, Muslim minorities, and anyone else that refuses to bow to their oppression, from the Tomb of Jonah in Mosul to Yazidi shrines in the Sinjar region and the historical site of Hijra, ISIS is trying to rewrite history. We have seen this tactic before—the Bamiyan Buddhas destroyed by the Taliban in Afghanistan, the Nazi destruction of Jewish religious property during World War II. We cannot allow another vicious group to reshape our record of the past. We need to cut off the profits ISIS gets from trafficking looted artifacts and to ramp up our efforts to save cultural property from destruction.

A few weeks ago, this committee unanimously passed the Protect and Preserve International Cultural Property Act which I introduced with Representative Smith, Chairman Royce and Representative Keating. This bill would help save cultural property from ISIS' campaign and we need to get this bill to the President's desk. We also need to stay focused on bringing relief to those living under the yoke of ISIS. I hope our witnesses can shed some light on what religious minorities living under ISIS control need the most.

The administration's response to degrade and destroy ISIS is a good start, but it is a start. The United States has worked to cut off financial support to ISIS; to stem the flow of foreign fighters; to deliver robust humanitarian assistance; to provide military support to our partners including through U.S. and coalition air strikes; and to push back against the violent ideology promoted by ISIS. But as we will hear today, people are still suffering in ISIS-held territory, and I hope today's testimony will underscore for my colleagues the need to pass a new authorization for the use of military force or AUMF. I have said this before and I will say it again and again and again until Congress acts on its responsibility and passes a new authorization.

And finally, I want to say that some of us are wearing red today. I am wearing a red tie and my good friend Ileana Ros-Lehtinen is wearing a red blouse, and we are doing this because we want to focus on the girls who have disappeared under Boko Haram. While Boko Haram is not ISIS, it is certainly affiliated. Their attacks are just as brutal and its terrorism all around the world and we need to stand up in this Congress and show that we will thwart it in any way possible. And I hope my colleagues will also wear red.

So once again I thank our witnesses and I look forward to hearing your testimony. And thank you, Mr. Chairman, for your leadership as always.

Chairman ROYCE. Thank you, Mr. Engel. Our panel that we are joined by here today include Sister Diana Momeka. She is a member of the Dominican Sisters of Saint Catherine of Siena located in Mosul, Iraq. Sister Diana, who was one of many thousands forced from their homes by an ISIS offensive last year, has been involved in providing assistance to other internally displaced Iraqis currently residing in Erbil and raising awareness of the plight of minorities displaced from Nineveh.

Ms. Jacqueline Isaac is the vice president of Roads of Success, a nonprofit organization dedicated to empowering women and minorities in the Middle East. Ms. Isaac's work has included refugee aid missions and helping families of victims in Iraq and in Jordan and in Egypt.

Ms. Hind Kabawat is the director of Interfaith Peacebuilding at the Center for World Religions, Diplomacy and Conflict Resolution for George Mason University. Ms. Kabawat has trained hundreds of Syrians in multi-faith collaboration, civil society development, women's empowerment, and in negotiation skills throughout the Middle East including in Aleppo, Syria.

Dr. Katharyn Hanson is a fellow at Penn Cultural Heritage Center for the University of Pennsylvania Museum specializing in the protection of cultural heritage specifically on the threats to Mesopotamian architectural sites in Iraq and in Syria. Dr. Hanson recently served as the program director for the Archaeological Site Preservation Program at the Iraqi Institute for the Conservation of Antiquities and Heritage in Erbil.

Without objection, the witnesses' full prepared statements will be made part of the record. Members are going to have 5 calendar days to submit statements and questions and any extraneous material they might want to put into the record.

And with that, Sister Diana, please summarize your remarks. And Sister Diana, she will push that red button there for you there.

STATEMENT OF SISTER DIANA MOMEKA, OP, DOMINICAN SISTERS OF SAINT CATHERINE OF SIENA, MOSUL, IRAQ

Sister MOMEKA. Thank you. Thank you, Chairman Royce and distinguished members of the committee for inviting me today to share my views on Ancient Communities Under Attack: ISIS's War on Religious Minorities.

Chairman ROYCE. Sister, I am going to suggest you move the microphone right in front there and just project a little bit. Thank you.

Sister MOMEKA. Okay, thank you. In November 2009, a bomb was detonated at our convent in Mosul. Five sisters were in the building at the time and they were lucky to have escaped unharmed. Our Prioress, Sister Maria Hanna, asked for protection from local civilian authorities but the pleas went unanswered. As such, she had no choice but to move us to Qaraqosh.

Then on June 10th, 2014, the so-called Islamic State in Iraq and Syria, or ISIS, invaded the Nineveh Plain which is where Qaraqosh is located. Starting with the city of Mosul, ISIS overran one city and town after another giving the Christians of the region three choices: Convert to Islam; pay a tribute, a jizya, to ISIS; leave their city, cities like Mosul, with nothing more than the clothes on their back. As this horror spread throughout the Nineveh Plain, by August 6, 2014, Nineveh was empty of Christians, and sadly, for the first time since the seventh century A.D., no church bells rang for mass in the Nineveh Plain.

From June 2014 forward, more than 120,000 people found themselves displaced and homeless in the Kurdistan region of Iraq leaving behind their heritage and all they had worked for over the centuries. This uprooting, this theft of everything that the Christians owned, displaced them body and soul, stripping away their humanity and dignity.

To add insult to injury, the initiatives and actions of both the Iraqi and Kurdish Governments were at best modest and slow.

Apart from allowing Christians to enter their region, the Kurdish Government did not offer any aid either financial or material.

I understand the great strain that these events have placed on Baghdad and Erbil. However, it has been almost a year and Christian Iraqi citizens are still in dire need of help. Many people spent days and weeks in the street before they found shelter in tents, schools, and halls. Thankfully, the church in the Kurdistan region stepped forward and cared for the displaced Christians, doing her very best to handle this disaster. Church buildings were opened to accommodate the people, food and non-food items were provided to meet the immediate needs of the people, and medical health service were also provided. Moreover, the Church put out a call and many humanitarian organizations answered with aid for thousands of people in need.

Presently we are grateful for what has been done, with most people now sheltered in small prefabricated containers or some homes. Though better than living on the streets or in the abandoned buildings, these small units are few in number and are crowded with three families, each with multiple people often accommodated in one unit. This of course increases tension and conflict even within the same family.

There are many who say, why don't the Christians just leave Iraq and move to another country and be done with it? To this question we would respond, why should we leave our country? What have we done? The Christians of Iraq are the first people of the land. You read about us in the Old Testament of the Bible. Christianity came to Iraq from the very earliest days through the preaching and witness of Saint Thomas and others of the Apostles and church elders. While our ancestors experienced all kinds of persecution, they stayed in their land, building a culture that has served humanity for ages.

We as Christians do not want or deserve to leave or be forced out of our country any more than you would want to leave or be forced out of yours. But the current persecution that our community if facing is the most brutal in our history. Not only have we been robbed of our homes, property and land, but our heritage is being destroyed as well. ISIS has and continues to demolish and bomb our churches, cultural artifacts and sacred places like Mar Behnam and his Sister, a fourth century monastery, and St. George's Monastery in Mosul.

Uprooted and forcefully displaced, we have realized that ISIS plans to evacuate the land of Christians and wipe the earth clean of any evidence that we ever existed. This is cultural and human genocide. The only Christians that remain in the Nineveh Plain are those who are held as hostages.

To restore and to rebuild the Christian community in Iraq the following needs are urgent: Liberating our homes from ISIS and helping us return; a coordinated efforts to rebuild what was destroyed—roads, water and electrical supplies, and buildings including our churches and monasteries; encouraging enterprises that contribute to the building of Iraq and inter-religious dialogue. This could be through schools, academics and pedagogical projects.

I am but one small person, a victim myself of ISIS and all of its brutality. Coming here has been difficult for me. As a religious sister I am not comfortable with the media and so much attention. But I am here and I am here to ask you, to implore you for the sake of our common humanity to help us. Stand with us, as we as Christians have stood with all the people of the world, and help us. We want nothing more than to go back to our lives. We want nothing more than to go home. Thank you and God bless you.

[The prepared statement of Sister Momeka follows:]

Sister Diana Momeka

Dominican Sisters of St. Catherine of Siena, Mosul, Iraq

House Foreign Affairs Committee

May 13, 2015

Ancient Communities Under Attack: ISIS's War on Religious Minorities

Thank you Chairman Royce and distinguished Members of the Committee, for inviting me today to share my views on Ancient Communities Under Attack: ISIS's War on Religious Minorities. I am Sister Diana Momeka of the Dominican Sisters of St. Catherine of Siena, Mosul, Iraq. I'd like to request that my complete testimony be entered in to the Record.

In November 2009, a bomb was detonated at our convent in Mosul. Five sisters were in the building at the time and they were lucky to have escaped unharmed. Our Prioress, Sister Maria Hanna, asked for protection from local civilian authorities but the pleas went unanswered. As such, she had no choice but to move us to Qaraqosh.

Then on June 10, 2014, the so-called Islamic State in Iraq and Syria or ISIS, invaded the Nineveh Plain, which is where Qaraqosh is located. Starting with the city of Mosul, ISIS overran one city and town after another, giving the Christians of the region three choices: **1.) convert to Islam, 2.) pay a tribute (Al-Jizya) to ISIS or 3.) leave their cities (like Mosul) with nothing more than the clothes on their back.**

As this horror spread throughout the Nineveh Plain, by August 6, 2014, Nineveh was emptied of Christians, and sadly, for the first time since the seventh century AD, no church bells rang for Mass in the Plain of Nineveh.

From June 2014 forward, more than a hundred and twenty thousand (120,000+) people found themselves displaced and homeless in the Kurdistan Region of Iraq, leaving behind their heritage and all they had worked for over the centuries. This uprooting, this theft of everything that the Christians owned, displaced them body and soul, stripping away their humanity and dignity.
To add insult to injury, the initiatives and actions of both the Iraqi and Kurdish governments were at best modest and slow. Apart from allowing Christians to enter their region, the Kurdish government did not offer any aid either financial or material. I understand the great strain that these events have placed on Baghdad and Erbil however, it has been almost a year and Christian Iraqi citizens are still in dire need of help. Many people spent days and weeks in the streets before they found shelter in tents, schools and halls. Thankfully, the Church in the Kurdistan region stepped forward and cared for the displaced Christians, doing her very best to handle the

disaster. Church buildings were opened to accommodate the people; food and non-food items were provided to meet the immediate needs of the people; and medical health services were also provided. Moreover, the Church put out a call and many humanitarian organizations answered with aid for the thousands of people in need.

Presently, we are grateful for what has been done, with most people now sheltered in small prefabricated containers or some homes. Though better than living on the street or in an abandoned building, these small units are few in number and are crowded with three families, each with multiple people, often accommodated in one unit. This of course increases tensions and conflict, even within the same family.

There are many who say "Why don't the Christians just leave Iraq and move to another country and be done with it?" To this question we would respond, "Why should we leave our country – what have we done?"

The Christians of Iraq are the first people of the land. You read about us in the Old Testament of the Bible. Christianity came to Iraq from the very earliest days through the preaching and witness of St Thomas and others of the Apostles and Church Elders.

While our ancestors experienced all kinds of persecution, they stayed in their land, building a culture that has served humanity for the ages. We, as Christians, do not want, or deserve to leave or be forced out of our country any more than you would want to leave or be forced out of yours.

But the current persecution that our community is facing is the most brutal in our history. Not only have we been robbed of our homes, property and land, but our heritage is being destroyed as well. ISIS has and continues to demolish and bomb our churches, cultural artifacts and sacred places like Mar Behnam and his Sister Sara, a fourth century monastery and St. Georges Monastery in Mosul.

Uprooted and forcefully displaced, we have realized that ISIS' plan is to evacuate the land of Christians and wipe the earth clean of any evidence that we ever existed. This is cultural and human genocide. The only Christians that remain in the Plain of Nineveh are those who are held as hostages.

The loss of the Christian Community from the Plain of Nineveh has placed the whole region on the edge of a terrible catastrophe. Christians have for centuries been the bridge that connects Eastern and Western cultures. Destroying this bridge will leave an isolated, inculturated conflict zone emptied of cultural and religious diversity. Through our presence as Christians, we're called to be a force for good, for peace, for connection between cultures.

To restore, repair and rebuild the Christian community in Iraq, the following needs are urgent:

1. Liberating our homes from ISIS and helping us return.

2. A coordinated effort to rebuild what was destroyed – roads, water and electrical supplies, and buildings, including our churches and monasteries.

3. Encouraging enterprises that contribute to the rebuilding of Iraq and inter-religious dialogue. This could be through schools, academics and pedagogical projects.

I am but one, small person – a victim myself of ISIS and all of its brutality. Coming here has been difficult for me – as a religious sister I am not comfortable with the media and so much attention. But I am here and I am here to ask you, to implore you for the sake of our common humanity to help us. Stand with us as we, as Christians, have stood with all the people of the world and help us. We want nothing more than to go back to our lives; we want nothing more than to go home.

Thank you and God bless you

Chairman Royce. Thank you, Sister.
Ms. Isaac?

STATEMENT OF MS. JACQUELINE ISAAC, VICE PRESIDENT, ROADS OF SUCCESS

Ms. Isaac. Honorable Chairman Royce, Ranking Member Engel and distinguished members of this committee, I am honored to be here today. Thank you so much for having a crucial hearing that really is a matter of life or death.

I am not talking to you as an attorney, I am not talking as a politician, I am talking about being a human being who has been on the front lines. I have been to Sinjar Mountain. I have met the girls that have been kidnapped and raped by ISIS. And I am telling you that we need to give them seeds of hope, seeds of hope to know that they can live and thrive in their home. I am here because I promised these people, my friends across the world that I would be their voices today.

Here are their narratives. I am here today because of a women I met named Ecklas. Ecclas was in Mosul at home at night and out of nowhere ISIS came in and said, you have two choices. You either convert to Islam or you pay the jizya. She gave them the money and she said give me 1 minute because my daughter is in the bathroom taking a shower. I am just going to get her out. They said, you don't have 1 second. They took a torch, they lit the house starting from the bathroom where she was taking a shower. Ecklas picked up her daughter Rita and she thought she could take her to the hospital. She had fourth degree burns. But Rita died in her arms.

I am here today because of Joy, an 11-years-old paralyzed kid from the neck down. ISIS found him in Sinjar town. They thought that he was useless to society so they picked him up with 190 other paralyzed and elderly people and they threw him in the borders of Syria.

But in the midst of all this darkness, I see that there is light. Light can break through the darkness, and we need to take our role as human beings, push them and help them to survive and thrive. Let me tell you what happened to Joy. The heroes of today, the Peshmerga army, found him with the other 190 and they rescued them. And today they are living in safety, and the Peshmerga army who is out there risking their lives are doing this on a constant basis. They are constantly rescuing the innocent.

One of those innocent girls that I met, I don't want to disclose her name for privacy purposes. She was 15 years old. And in one night in Sinjar town ISIS came in and took her, with a group of hundreds of girls, into a broken down building, and ISIS came in and they started to trade, trading her off, categorizing these girls as merchandise depending on whether they were beautiful in their eyes, how old they were, whether they were virgins or not, literally treating them like merchandise. She was sent off and she was being raped on a constant basis. And she decided to make an escape. She believed that she rather die trying. She believed that somebody out there, another human being would help her if she made an escape. And in one night she broke out of a window and she started to make a run for it.

My brave friend went hours hiking on the top of the Sinjar mountain, but ISIS came back for her and took her back. When she went to that house they starved her, they beat her, and again she said I would rather die trying. ISIS forgot to fix the window they broke and she made a run for it, and this time she made it to the very top.

And who was there to stand by her side? The Peshmerga army, the Kurdish Regional Government who have already rescued at least 480 girls and children, 30 of which are impregnated. Many of those that have been impregnated by ISIS committed suicide. The others who received the counseling, who received that push of hope, that seed that each of us can provide, started to dream again, started to see a future.

Today I ask for four things. I ask that we support the brave Peshmerga army who is resisting terror at the front lines. They are not just fighting to protect their land. They are not fighting to preserve the religious minorities alone. They are fighting for the entire world. Second, I ask that we provide humanitarian assistance, more and more of it, because today there is about 2 million refugees and IDPs living in the Kurdistan Regional Government region and they need our support. They need psychological counseling to deal with the trauma. We are talking about a future generation here. Let us help them get the support that they need. Let us help the brave government that is on the front lines, the army that are truly the boots on the ground. I ask that we recognize their amazing rescue efforts.

And lastly, I ask of you to help their partners. Countries like Egypt, who is now taking hundreds of thousands of Syrians in their own land. Countries like Egypt, when President el-Sisi had heard that 21 Christians were killed in Libya acted immediately at deploying those air strikes. Countries like Jordan, which is taking in hundreds of thousands of IDPs and refugees and also fighting on those front lines. Let us support them because this is a matter of national security. It is not about them. It is about all of us together.

I have a video if we have a moment to show these girls are going to share with us their stories.

Chairman ROYCE. Without objection.

[Video.]

Ms. ISAAC. These girls have hope. They have hope that we are going to help them. Let us all do it together. Thank you.

[The prepared statement of Ms. Isaac follows:]

Testimony to the U.S. House of Representatives Foreign Affairs Committee

May 11, 2015

By Jacqueline Isaac, Esq.

Vice President, <u>Roads of Success</u>, *Los Angeles, California*

For over a decade, I have been involved in supporting victims of crisis and; advancing religious minorities' and women's rights across the Middle East. Since the emergence of ISIS, I have traveled to Northern Iraq several times through *Roads of Success, a non-profit organization. Our missions* included: (1) trucking medical supplies and basic necessities through the warring zones in Iraq and distributing the items to internally displaced persons in camps where survivors crowd into tents and in the field, such as to the Yazidis on top of the Sinjar mountain; (2) holding workshops in an effort to heal, restore and empower the girls who have been raped and tortured while in ISIS captivity, and (3) spending time on the frontlines with the Peshmerga army (military forces of Iraqi-Kurdistan) witnessing their needs on the ground.

I also visited the Egyptian families of 15 of the 21 Coptic Christians beheaded by ISIS in Libya. I delivered to His Holiness Pope Tawadros II of Alexandria, the condolences of Foreign Affairs Committee, Chairman Royce who wrote,

> *"Sadly, ISIS is bringing this barbarity across the region-beheading and crucifying those who don't share their dark ideology. The threat from this group seems to grow by the day. It will take all of us, working together, to focus our efforts to ensure this evil is defeated.... As Chairman of the House Foreign Affairs Committee, I'm committed to ensuring that the rights of religious minorities across the Middle East are recognized and protected[.]"*

To preserve ancient religious minority communities and protect those fleeing from ISIS, I recommend the following:

Directly provide conventional weapons, support services, and training to the military forces of the Kurdistan Regional Government for use exclusively against ISIS;

Increase humanitarian assistance to the Kurdistan Regional Government for its care of millions of refugees and internally displaced persons in the Iraqi-Kurdistan region;

Highlight the Kurdistan Regional Government's crucial role in rescuing the innocent and beating back the menace that ISIS is to humanity;

Increase military and economic support for our other allies in the region who are working to defeat ISIS, particularly Jordan and Egypt.

In my most recent visit of March 2015, I spent significant time with those displaced and/or affected by ISIS in Iraq and Egypt. It is clear to me that ISIS aims to eliminate all religious minorities in the region; ISIS continues to destroy the towns and livelihoods of the ancient Yazidi, Christian and other religious minority communities. The survivors are calling on the world to save their ancient communities from complete destruction.

Although ISIS intended to destroy through enslavement, rape and torture, they could not capture the souls of the courageous and resilient survivors I encountered. Their hope to remain in the region depends on the brave and courageous leaders of the Kurdistan Regional Government and on those surrounding safe havens such as Jordan and Egypt. I observed a common theme of gratitude by the displaced towards the governments who managed to create safe havens that survivors, at least for now, call home.

As the people of Iraqi-Kurdistan continue to prove themselves against ISIS, it is the responsibility of decent governments around the world to help make the burden of this battle bearable. As ISIS forced millions to flee across Northern Iraq, the Kurdistan Regional Government took it upon itself to provide shelter, food, medical care and protection to the displaced. Today, the Iraqi-Kurdistan Region has become a safe haven to Shia Muslims, Sunni Muslims, Armenians, Assyrians, Chaldeans, Syriac, Kakai, Shabk, Turkmen and Yazidis-a place of equality, religious freedom and most importantly, safety.

After witnessing the dedication to the displaced of Kurdistan Regional Government leaders and their local workers on the ground, I suggest the following measures:

1. **Provide a direct transfer to the Kurdistan Regional Government of conventional weapons, support services, and training to help defeat ISIS**-The brave Peshmerga army, one-third of which are women fighters, defend the innocent without essential weaponry or even basic equipment and have been scarcely paid salaries due to budget issues. They desperately need sophisticated U.S. military weaponry to help them secure their own land, protect religious minorities and defend from ISIS's advance. All of the other noteworthy goals-development, education, infrastructure, the strengthening of the rule of law-are the fruits of a basic level of security. In the present crisis, that security must be won by the force of arms.

2. **Increase humanitarian support**-The Kurdistan Regional Government has exhausted most of the humanitarian resources that were available in the region-As they continue to welcome more innocent persons fleeing from the terrors of ISIS while their poverty rate continues to rise and government workers go unpaid for long periods. The U.S. should also call upon the world community to do more in providing tangible humanitarian assistance.

3. Highlight the rescue efforts of the Kurdistan Regional Government - Left with the horrid memories of rape and torture, some of the women and girls once enslaved by ISIS ended their own lives, however, the Kurdistan Regional Government and its friends, are doing everything in their power to help the survivors of those who were in ISIS's captivity. The Kurdistan Regional Government is calling on world governments and NGOs to assist them in the aid, psychological healing, and empowerment of the girls and children who have escaped the horrors of ISIS in Iraq. As a response to the call for help, *Roads of Success* brought a team of U.S. trauma experts to Iraq to aid the victims. I witnessed the transformational growth the girls experienced just after a few hours of counseling and being reminded of their value and purpose, a stark difference after ISIS had sold them as merchandise, classifying their price according to age, beauty, and virginity.

President Masoud Barzani has publicly reported on the Kurdistan Regional Government's rescue of 1,300 people and he pledges that the government will continue to do everything in it's power to rescue thousands that remain captive. It is crucial for the United States to highlight the strides made by the Kurdistan Regional Government 's rescue missions while continuing to condemn ISIS's brutal attacks-particularly those against girls and children.

4. Increase military and economic support of our allies in the region such as Jordan and Egypt in their fight against ISIS- By strengthening our security and economic cooperation with frontline partners like Jordan and Egypt, as well as the Kurdistan Regional Government, we promote our own national security by helping them destroy the nerve center of ISIS's international operations.

Last week's recent shooting in Texas, likely accredited to ISIS, is one of the many reasons to arm the Kurdistan Regional Government. This incident on our own land is a concrete example of the way the presence of ISIS in the Middle East provides a focus and sense of mission to lone wolves all over the world. Keeping disaffected types everywhere from unifying is a key element to keeping down their violence. ISIS's operation zone in the Middle East is a nerve center for inciting terrorism everywhere, just as Al Qaeda's presence in Afghanistan was in pre-2001.

The Kurdistan Regional Government's track record proves that the people of Iraqi-Kurdistan are reliable friends to the United States and standard bearers of decency in the region-They have acted with humanity and bravery to protect innocent civilians fleeing from terror-regardless of race, creed or religion.

When I had the honor to meet with Iraqi-Kurdistan President Masoud Barzani last week, he reaffirmed his dedication publicly to all religious minorities in the Kurdistan Regional Government region, personally urging them not to flee Iraq but to stay. President Barzani addressed religious minorities, stating via interpretation, "We do not want any of you to think about leaving the country, going to be asylum seekers abroad. I assure that we will be together. Either we live freely in our country or we will die together. "

There are two basic reasons that the United States must do more in the fight against ISIS, particularly, when one considers the plight of innocent people in ISIS's group. First , it is in America's national security interest to see ISIS defeated, both as an idea and as a military movement. Second, the preservation of human life and property-especially of allies like the people of Iraqi-Kurdistan, Jordanians and Iraqi citizens- is commensurate with our highest ideals.

It is true the U.S. can not do everything at all places, at all times, but this crisis is different. We cherish ethnic and religious diversity; ISIS hates it. The U.S. wants peace and security for the entire region; peace for ALL law-abiding people, whether Sunni, Shia, Kurd or from Iraq or Syria's many religious minorities. However, the present crisis may see entire communities purged from the land at the hands of ISIS.

What makes this situation particularly compelling is the role the U.S. has played in greater Iraq over the past decade; our good-will attempt to protect women, religious minorities and sectarian communities through security development, and education. Unfortunately, at present, many of the tools we left behind to assist the Iraqi security forces have been appropriated by ISIS and are being used to terrorize the population. We can do more to stop this scourge.

It is imperative for the U.S. to assist the Iraqi-Kurdistan army now, not only to secure their own land, but to stop ISIS's terrorist acts and recruitment. It is in our national security to act now, and help remove this menace from the world.

Chairman ROYCE. Thank you, Jacqueline.
Ms. Kabawat.

STATEMENT OF MS. HIND KABAWAT, DIRECTOR OF INTER-FAITH PEACEBUILDING, CENTER FOR WORLD RELIGIONS, DIPLOMACY, AND CONFLICT RESOLUTION, GEORGE MASON UNIVERSITY

Ms. KABAWAT. Thank you Chairman Royce, Ranking Member Engel, and other members of the committee. I am honored to be here today and speak to you about the status of religious minorities in Syria, a subject very close to my heart. Growing up as a Christian in Syria, I was surrounded by rich multi-religious history. I have lived much of my life on road called Straight Street, a road so ancient it was mentioned in the Bible.

Today it saddens me to see the Christians in Syria paying a very high price for this senseless war. They have been running from their villages and homes. They are displaced. Their churches are being destroyed. A report by my colleague Dr. Wael al-Alelj lists all the destroyed churches in Syria including those destroyed by ISIS and by the regime.

Protecting Christians is essential. But while I urge you to do whatever is possible to protect minorities and Christians from ISIS, I would like to remind you that ISIS is killing any and every Muslim who oppose them, just as the Muslims and minorities are killed by Assad regime. My friend Jamila a very religious Muslim from Raqqa was threatened by ISIS and escaped at night to Turkey fearing death. Some Sunni tribes have suffered massive losses to ISIS. For example, ISIS forces killed more than 500 youth of Shaitat tribes in 1 day last year. Women and children live in constant, traumatizing fear afraid of recruitment by ISIS.

As a Christian, I cannot request safety for my Christian community without worrying about others. Yes, we need to create safe havens for minorities and all groups threatened by ISIS. It is monumental and worthwhile tasks. And when selecting these areas, geography is essential. Areas close to Turkish and Jordan's borders are the best candidates because of the guarantee that those borders will remain secure.

Additionally, an important component of safe havens will be the proximity to protect zones by first liberating all ISIS controlled cities in these zones. The security of the safe haven will be easier to maintain. In the last 3 years, I have regularly visited the refugee camps in Turkey, Jordan and IDP camp in Zaatari, in Idlib, Jabal al-Zawiya and others. The women there wants to go back home. They want to live without fear of crate and barrel bombs.

As we discuss religious minorities, I urge you also to consider the need of women who have been marginalized as well. They are the key to peace process and the key to establishing community that provides support for one another across sectarian lines. Empowering local councils to deliver social services is another essential component of establishing safe havens for all Syrians. The base guarantee for the prosperities of minorities in the Middle East is in a democracy that accords everyone the same right and privileges regardless of their ethnic or religious background.

The message to minorities in the Middle East should be one of inclusion, equipping and encouraging them to be part of the democratic process which is the only possibility to defeat extremism and dictatorship in our country. Thank you and I look forward for your questions.

[The prepared statement of Ms. Kabawat follows:]

Testimony before the House Committee on Foreign Affairs
"Ancient Communities Under Attack: ISIS's War on Religious Minorities"

Hind Kabawat
Director of Interfaith Peacebuilding
Center for World Religions, Diplomacy, and Conflict Resolution at George Mason University

Rayburn House Office Building, Washington, DC
May 13, 2015

Chairman Royce, Ranking Member Engel, and Members of the Committee – I would like to thank you for inviting me here to discuss the status of religious minorities under ISIS. I am truly honored by your invitation and grateful for the concern that this committee continues to show for all of the Syrian people.

I am a Syrian Christian from Damascus. I raised my children there. My husband still lives there, in our home in the old city - on a street called Straight, which is mentioned in the Bible dozens of times. My children grew up playing with their Muslim and Christian friends. They learned that Syria was a place of harmony for people of different religions to live peacefully; to coexist; and to set an example for communities worldwide.

ISIS's ASSAULT ON SYRIA

The threat of ISIS has endangered Muslims and Christians alike, all of whom have been victim to its brutal treatment of those who do not follow its cruel and deeply flawed interpretation of Islam. Religious minority communities have been particularly threatened and abused; such violence is, as Chairman Royce described it, truly sickening. In addition to its broad targeting and killing of Christians, minorities, and Muslims who do not fit their extremist codes, ISIS has in particular destroyed the lives of countless women and girls in a display of enslavement, rape, and horror that has no precedent for us in Syria. Women and girls are thus subject to horror from all sides.

Beyond its barbaric human rights violations, ISIS has further sought to destroy these communities by erasing their cultural and religious heritage – attacking churches, mosques, shrines, and ancient sites. By targeting Assyrian archaeology, ISIS goes beyond ethnic and religious cleansing to further wipe out any historical trace of the people it has displaced. Because these sites harken back to a flourishing and pluralistic past that legitimizes the histories of religious minorities, such sites are seen as a threat to ISIS and are summarily destroyed. The group believes that it cannot control the future until it controls the past.

The outcome of ISIS's campaign to cleanse Iraq and Syria of these indigenous minority communities has been widespread success in the areas where they have most forcefully concentrated their efforts. In cities where ISIS is now firmly in control, such as Raqqa, religious minorities have been largely driven out, with the exception of some still in hiding in small pockets of these areas. The areas where the fate of religious minorities has yet to be decided are those locations where ISIS has not yet gained a decisive victory. A two-pronged approach is needed in these cities: to continue to aggressively combat and counter ISIS while simultaneously protecting the citizens they seek to conquer, focusing specifically on the most vulnerable among them.

CREATING SAFE HAVENS FOR SYRIANS

Nowhere in Syria is safe – especially not for religious minorities. Creating safe havens where Syrians fleeing ISIS-controlled and -contested cities can seek refuge inside the country is of utmost importance as a way to manage the conflict in the short term. The first step in doing so is to liberate the cities around the safe haven to create a buffer zone between the location of the haven and the reach of ISIS. The ideal would be to build havens where those escaping from ISIS can be independent, safe, and in charge of their own defense, and to establish fair laws for everyone. As part of their protection, these safe havens must without question be no-fly zones that are also secured by a strong, moderate army on the ground.

Women are the most effective guarantors of peace in any society. By providing safe havens for families, we can ensure that women from across the spectrum of minorities will help each other and their communities. In my work with the Center for World Religions, Diplomacy, and Conflict Resolution, I have managed and been witness to numerous joint operations of training between minority and majority women who protect each other from the violence that threatens them from all sides. The best way to build these safe havens is to build them in cooperation with established networks of women and men – minorities and majorities – who have a track record of working together and protecting each other. Such alliances are the best guarantees of safety, security, and general welfare and serve as avenues from immediate crisis management to near-term solutions.

LOCATIONS AND CHARACTERISTICS OF SAFE HAVENS

There are certain regions of the country, such as Hasake, a city in the province of Jazira in northeastern Syria, that will be particularly helpful places to set up a safe haven. The area from Tell Abiad to Aleppo would function as a buffer zone for the Jazira safe haven: since it is protected by the Turkish border in the north and moderate groups in Aleppo, the only points of compromise for this zone are the south and the east. ISIS controls Manbij, which is part of the proposed zone and would need to be liberated in order for the zone to be effective. Raqqa is far south enough that the ISIS forces there are unlikely to attempt to penetrate the buffer zone as long as it is adequately protected by the moderate opposition. Because there are many minorities, including Christians, Kurds, and Assyrians, in Hasake and Qamishli, this far corner of northeastern Syria is an ideal location to establish the first large-scale safe haven for all people that can then serve as a model and testing ground for other areas.

Key to the maintenance and success of safe havens is the policy of inclusion. Our goal should be to guarantee the best safety possible for the greatest number of Syrians possible, bringing together men and women from all ethnic and religious groups who can easily and quickly gain access to the safe haven area. Singling out a specific ethnic or religious group to protect more earnestly than others would be damaging to Syria's security in the long term and preclude a return to the coexistence that has been a hallmark of Syria's long history. Thus Hasake and Qamishli offer us the best site for a safe haven not only because of their geographic location but also because they are home to Christians, Muslims, and all other communities that we should seek to protect: all Syrians.

LOCAL COUNCILS IN SAFE HAVENS AS THE KEY TO SUCCESS

Another essential element of the creation of safe havens is the need to maintain them through the provision of social services and the guarantee of good governance. Local councils supported by the moderate opposition have for years acted as the sole governing bodies in some areas. Such councils are democratically elected and have a demonstrated commitment to minorities and the safeguarding of women's and human rights. I have personally attended some of their meetings in several liberated areas and was welcomed as a Christian and a woman who trained them in capacity building and conflict resolution skills. One council worked closely with our organization to release a priest from Idlib who had been taken captive; after Idlib was liberated, that same council guaranteed that they would protect the safety of the Christians there.

NECESSITY OF SOCIAL SERVICES AND TRAUMA SUPPORT

Support for these local councils is the best hope for maintaining regions of Syria that will be safe for Christians to return to. However, these groups are significantly underfunded in comparison to ISIS and the al-Nusra Front, both of which have extremely well-funded social programs that fill the void of social services that have not existed in these areas since the start of the revolution. Providing significant funding and support to these civilian-run councils will pave the way for a smoother transition to democracy and ensure that Syrians committed to a pluralistic Syria where everyone is respected are empowered for the future.

In order to compete with the social services that other groups provide, local councils in safe havens, buffer zones, and all liberated areas of Syria must be equipped to implement development projects that give their citizens a stake in their community's future and a means of self-sufficiency. Such work should include the building and maintenance of hospitals and schools and significant opportunities for agricultural and other development work. Many of these regions have lacked electricity and clean water for much of the last few years, while ISIS is able to provide these services for people in the areas it controls. Local councils need funding and capacity building to secure these resources and to rebuild municipal buildings that have been destroyed in the war. Centers to support community and family life and trauma healing are without question essential to communities in every corner of Syria. The men, women, and children of my country have been traumatized by the attacks they have experienced and the immense losses that they have sustained. If we wait until the war is over to begin addressing such widespread and systematic trauma, we will have lost an entire generation of Syrians who are now growing up amidst horror and war with no outlets for trauma healing or PTSD support. By guaranteeing social services beyond the mere basics of medical care and clean water, we not only position the local councils to surpass ISIS in terms of capability but also proactively work for the long-term good of the Syrian people to ensure that the atrocities of the last four years do not color the future of this country.

PROVIDING FOR SYRIA'S FUTURE THROUGH A PROVEN INCLUSIVE APPROACH

ISIS, of course, is not the only warring faction in Syria that has targeted religious minorities. The regime of Bashar Al Assad has damaged and destroyed churches – Catholic, Orthodox, and Armenian – all over the country by directly targeting them, with no regard for the collateral damage. Only last year, government forces attacked the Lady of Peace Roman Catholic Church in Homs for the sixth time by planting a landmine inside the church, which exploded and killed the Christian man inside.

Just as minorities in Syria cannot be protected without also addressing the safety of the majority, ISIS cannot be controlled and defeated without addressing the terrorism of Bashar Al Assad and his government. Safe havens are a short-term solution to protect minorities, women, and other Syrian civilians from brutal death at the hands of ISIS; but without a long-term political solution to end the war and stop the violence, these same citizens will face death at the hands of the regime regardless.

I have worked with Dr. Marc Gopin at the Center for World Religions, Diplomacy, and Conflict Resolution since 2004. Together we have trained hundreds of Syrians – Christians, Alawites, Muslims, and secular groups – in negotiation, civil society building, and conflict resolution skills. Before the revolution, we worked inside Syria; since the conflict began, we have continued to train Syrians from all parts of the country and those seeking refuge in Turkey and Jordan. In training and supporting these groups, we have found countless examples of Christians, Muslims, and all other minorities working together to protect their communities in the face of ISIS and the regime. Civil society organizations and women's groups bring together majority and minority communities: in Aleppo, for example, many churches have welcomed Muslims in need of medical attention, and Muslims are protecting and providing for the Christian nursing home there. These groups and individuals are not choosing sectarian divisions; instead, they choose the humanitarian side, as their faith and mine compels us to do.

The sustainability of protection for religious minorities can only be guaranteed by involving the majority and all other groups in securing these safe havens, providing administrative and governmental support in the form of local councils, and protecting the safe havens and their buffer zones. The safe havens themselves must be open to *all* citizens who would seek refuge there; if the West appears to favor minority groups – even though they are those most cruelly targeted by ISIS – such an approach would isolate and alienate my Christian community and sow seeds of future discord and resentment. Relationships and alliances among the different Syrian communities have survived four years of war and destruction and continue to work for the good of the Syrian people despite the enormous adversity they face. I ask you to take advantage of these incredible networks; to build them up and support them;

and to use them to protect all communities in the short term while working to ensure that a long-term political solution is brought about through principled and sustained diplomacy and negotiation.

ABOUT THE CENTER FOR WORLD RELIGIONS, DIPLOMACY, AND CONFLICT RESOLUTION

The Center for World Religions, Diplomacy, and Conflict Resolution (CRDC) is the flagship center for international conflict resolution practice at the School for Conflict Analysis and Resolution at George Mason University. CRDC seeks to engage emerging indigenous and global conflict resolvers, partner with them in innovative entrepreneurial growth, mobilize support for them, and create linkages between peacebuilders, citizen diplomats, students, business people and policy makers.

CRDC was founded in 2003 through a major gift commitment from the Catalyst Fund, which endowed the James H. Laue Chair in World Religions, Diplomacy, and Conflict Resolution and created CRDC to be directed by the Chair. In the twelve years since, CRDC has pioneered work in Syria and Afghanistan focusing on local peacebuilding, citizen diplomacy, and interfaith approaches to conflict resolution under the direction of Dr. Marc Gopin.

CRDC's goal is to inspire and generate successful incremental steps of positive change in intractable conflict situations that can become the basis for new approaches to diplomacy and foreign policy. Paths to positive change include civil society development through education in conflict resolution; peer mediation; innovative religious, spiritual, and cultural forms of conflict resolution; culturally effective methods of cooperation on development projects of benefit to all parties; and an integrated relationship between the world of such work and the world of policymakers and diplomats.

Chairman ROYCE. Thank you.
Thank you, Dr. Hanson.

STATEMENT OF KATHARYN HANSON, PH.D., FELLOW, PENN CULTURAL HERITAGE CENTER, UNIVERSITY OF PENNSYLVANIA MUSEUM

Ms. HANSON. Chairman Royce, Ranking Member Engel and members of the committee. Thank you for this opportunity to discuss ISIS's destruction of minority religious and cultural sites. ISIS's campaign of targeted extermination includes the erasure of the outward manifestations of minority religious culture which threatens these communities' way of life.

I study this subject as a Fellow at the Penn Cultural Heritage Center of the University of Pennsylvania Museum. But like others on this panel, I was in Erbil, Iraq, in August 2014, when ISIS advanced toward the Erbil Plain. As a program director at the Iraqi Institute for the Conservation of Antiquities and Heritage in Erbil, I was leading a course for heritage professionals from throughout the country—men and women of every religion. This training was interrupted and we departed abruptly shortly after air strikes began.

Despite this setback, the desire of Iraqi heritage professionals to protect the religious and cultural sites of the country remains strong. Based on my current research, experience in Iraq and consultation with Iraqi colleagues, I want to share some examples of ISIS's destruction. Slide 1 please.

Ms. HANSON. In July 2014 in Mosul, Iraq, ISIS destroyed the shrine of Nebi Yunus also known as the tomb of the prophet Jonah. An analysis of satellite imagery by the American Association for the Advancement of Sciences Geospatial Technologies Project where I am a visiting scholar confirmed this destruction. Slide 2 please.

This analysis also showed that ISIS removed all evidence of the shrine by clearing rubble and grading the site flat. In doing so, ISIS erased the physical presence of Nebi Yunus for the entire local religious community. Slide 3 please.

Dura-Europos is an archaeological site in Syria with uniquely preserved Roman provincial architecture. It includes the world's best preserved ancient Jewish synagogue and one of the earliest known Christian house chapels. The chapel dates to about 235 A.D. and contains the oldest known depiction of Jesus Christ. Slide 4 please.

The site has now been extensively looted and is currently under ISIS control. The before and after image analyzed analysis completed by the AAAS's geotech project demonstrates that over 76 percent of the site's surface has now been lost. Slide 5 please.

Two months ago I traveled to the Dohuk Governorate in Iraq which is adjacent to ISIS-held areas. I met with the director of the antiquities department to identify religious and cultural sites at risk. This site, Lalish, may be one of the only surviving Yazidi religious centers. Slide 6 please.

ISIS has released two videos that include the defacement of an ancient sculpture called the Lamassu. These are human-headed, winged bulls. In ancient times they represented the power of the

Neo-Assyrian empire from the ninth to seventh century B.C. Today, they serve as important symbols for Assyrian Christians. ISIS's defacement is thus intended to terrorize the present-day Iraqi Christian community while simultaneously destroying ancient artifacts.

In thinking about how we can address this destruction, I would like to offer three recommendations. First, we must prepare humanitarian assistance to religious and refugee communities as well as to displaced heritage professionals. In the near future I will return to Erbil, Iraq, with colleagues from the University of Pennsylvania Museum and the Smithsonian Institution and there we will work with our Iraqi colleagues to determine unmet emergency needs. More programs like this are necessary, and the U.S. Government should encourage new collaborations in the nonprofit sector.

Second, this committee should inquire into efforts to protect religious and other cultural sites during military actions against ISIS. There is a report that should shed some light on these efforts due in June 2015 thanks to a provision sponsored by Mr. Engel in the National Defense Authorization Act. I recommend that this committee scrutinize the report carefully for evidence that steps are being taken to avoid accidental air strikes on religious and cultural sites and that protection measures are incorporated into advisory rules and military trainings.

Finally, there is bipartisan legislation, the Protect and Preserve International Cultural Property Act introduced by Mr. Engel, Mr. Smith, Mr. Royce, and Mr. Keating. Its purpose is twofold. To bring together the agencies that have existing mandates to protect heritage, and to eliminate the financial incentive for entities such as ISIS to loot religious and cultural artifacts. I commend this committee for its bipartisan leadership on this bill, and I urge you to advocate for its final passage into law.

I would like to thank the chairman for convening this important hearing at a very critical juncture in the preservation of religious and cultural heritage. I am happy to answer any questions that you have.

[The prepared statement of Ms. Hanson follows:]

Testimony of
Katharyn Hanson Ph.D.
Fellow, Penn Cultural Heritage Center,
University of Pennsylvania Museum

Hearing: Ancient Communities Imperiled: ISIS's War on Religious Minorities
House Committee on Foreign Affairs
Wednesday, May 13, 2015

Statement

Chairman Royce, Ranking Member Engel, and members of the Committee, thank you for
this opportunity to testify before you on the impact of ISIS to the religious and cultural
heritage of minority groups in Iraq and Syria.

Minority religious heritage sites throughout ISIS held areas of Iraq and Syria have been
suffering enormous damage and face constant risk. The targeted extermination of
religious minorities by ISIS results in mass death and also the erasure of the outward
manifestations of the minority religious culture, threatening the continuity of their
religious practices.

I study this subject as a Fellow with the Penn Cultural Heritage Center at the University
of Pennsylvania Museum. But like others on this panel, I was in Erbil, Iraq in August
2014, when ISIS made its advances toward the Erbil plain. I was then serving as the
Program Director for the Archaeological Site Preservation Program at the Iraqi Institute
for the Conservation of Antiquities and Heritage in Erbil, Iraq, where I was leading a
course for heritage professionals from throughout the country—men and women of every
religious creed—who were working together to preserve the country's cultural sites. This
work was interrupted by ISIS, and we departed abruptly, shortly after airstrikes began.
However, the desire of Iraqi cultural heritage professionals to protect the religious and
cultural heritage of the country remains.

Based on my current research, my experience in Iraq, and my consultation with Iraqi
colleagues over the past several years, I want to share some examples of ISIS's targeted
and intentional damage to minority religious and cultural sites.

- According to media reports in July 2014, ISIS destroyed the shrine of Nebi Yunis,
  located in Mosul, Iraq and revered as the tomb of the Prophet Jonah. Subsequent
  analysis of satellite imagery by the American Association for the Advancement of
  Science's Geospatial Technologies Project, where I am a visiting scholar,
  demonstrated that this was indeed the case. However, this analysis also showed that
  ISIS went further, removing all evidence of the shrine by bringing in heavy trucks to
  clear the rubble and then grading the site flat. ISIS's activities erased the physical
  remains and memory of the Nebi Yunis' shrine completely, and likely damaged the
  buried remains of the site's earlier mosques, churches, and temples.

- Dura-Europos is often called the "Pompeii of the Desert" because this ancient archaeological site uniquely preserves ancient sacred architecture from the 3rd century BC onwards. Surviving structures include temples to ancient Greek and Mesopotamian gods as well as the world's best-preserved ancient Jewish synagogue and one of the earliest known Christian house chapels. The chapel contains the oldest known depiction of Jesus Christ and dates to about 235 AD. This site has now been extensively looted and is currently under ISIS control. The before and after image analysis completed by the American Association for the Advancement of Science's Geospatial Technologies Project demonstrates that some 76 percent of the site's surface area within the ancient city walls has now been looted.

- Two months ago, I traveled to the Dohuk Governorate in Iraq, which is adjacent to the ISIS-held Nineveh Governorate. While there, I met with the director of the Dohuk Antiquities Department about the minority religious and cultural sites at risk. To the best of our present knowledge, a number of Yazidi shrines have been destroyed since ISIS took control of Mosul and Sinjar. It now appears that Lalish may be one of the only surviving Yazidi religious centers in the region and is identified by the Dohuk Antiquities Department as the cultural site most at risk.

- In recent weeks, ISIS has released two videos showing the defacement of a particular type of ancient sculpture called a *lamassu*. These sculptures are human-headed winged bulls or lions made during the Neo-Assyrian Empire between the 9th and 7th century BC. While these statues represented the power of the Neo-Assyrian Empire in ancient times, today, they often serve as important symbols to the modern Assyrian Christian population. ISIS's defacement of a *lamassu* is therefore intended to terrorize the present-day Christian community while simultaneously destroying an ancient artifact.

In thinking about how we can address the intentional destruction of minority religious and cultural heritage, I would like to offer three recommendations of actions that can be taken now by the Committee and the U.S. Government.

- First, to the extent possible, we need to offer humanitarian assistance to religious and refugee communities as well as the displaced museum curators, librarians, archivists, and archaeologists who are working at great personal risk to protect religious and cultural heritage inside Iraq and Syria. In the near future, I will return to Erbil, Iraq with colleagues from the University of Pennsylvania Museum and the Smithsonian Institution, where we will be working with heritage professionals to determine what unmet emergency needs currently exist. We need more programs like this one to reach additional religious and refugee communities, and the U.S. Government should encourage new partnerships and collaborations to form in the non-profit sector on this issue.

- Second, this Committee should use its powers to inquire into the efforts by the Department of Defense to protect religious heritage and other cultural sites during action against ISIS. This Committee should further investigate as to whether the proper protections for religious and cultural heritage have been integrated into training for the Peshmerga, the Iraqi Army, and the Free Syrian Army. There is a report that should shed light on these efforts, which was required by Title XII, Subtitle E, Section 1273 of the National Defense Authorization Act for Fiscal Year 2015. This provision was sponsored by Mr. Engel, and the report due to be completed in June 2015. I recommend that this Committee scrutinize the report carefully for evidence that the Department of Defense has taken steps to avoid accidental air strikes on religious and cultural sites and incorporated protection measures into their advisory role with local stakeholders.

- Finally, there is bipartisan legislation on cultural heritage protection, the Protect and Preserve International Cultural Property Act, HR 1493, now pending in this Congress. Introduced by Mr. Engel, Mr. Smith, Mr. Royce, and Mr. Keating, the purpose of the legislation is twofold: first, it is designed to make the implementation of U.S. policies more effective by bringing together the various agencies that have an existing mandate to address international heritage protection; and, second, to eliminate the financial incentive for terrorist entities such as ISIS to loot religious heritage and archaeological sites by restricting the importation of such material into U.S. markets. I commend this Committee and its members for their bipartisan leadership in unanimously passing HR 1493, and I urge members of this Committee to advocate for its final passage into law.

I would like to thank the Chairman for convening this important hearing at a very critical juncture in the preservation of Iraq and Syria's religious and cultural heritage. I will be happy to answer any questions that you have.

Chairman ROYCE. Well, thank you, Dr. Hanson. That legislation by the way has been passed out of committee. It is on the floor and we are going to move it shortly. And I would just make a couple of observations. One is that this ISIS phenomenon, another way it could have been handled was when ISIS originally was in Raqqa, as they were leaving Raqqa, there were those of us on this committee as well as some of our Ambassadors overseas that suggested overwhelming U.S. air power hit the ISIS forces in Raqqa or hit the ISIS forces as they were leaving in their long caravan as they begin their attacks town by town by town, and we did not act from the air at that time. We allowed them to take some 14 major cities, culminating in taking Mosul, without the use of air power at the time to stop them while they were in these long columns.

Subsequently we began the process in this committee, bipartisan, to argue for arming the Kurds. Why? Because the Kurdish battalions were strung out on a 600-mile front with ISIS. They were the one effective force not just fighting ISIS but taking in behind their front lines Christians, Yazidis, other minorities, and willing to put themselves at risk to go into territory, ISIS-held, in order to rescue Yazidis and other minorities, and they were fighting with small arms fire against ISIS which had become the best financed terror group in the history of any terror organization because they took the Central Bank at Mosul and had at their disposal enormous wealth, and because they took weapons along the way.

So our efforts have gone on now, I would say, for 9 months to try to get into the hands of the Kurds the anti-tank missiles, the artillery, the long range mortars that they need on the battlefield. Thirty percent of these Kurdish battalions are females. They are women fighting on the front lines against ISIS and they are fighting without adequate equipment. And as you put it so well, they are fighting for civilization. Not just their own, for other religious minorities and, frankly, for a principle. And because of the pressure from Iran, pressure on Baghdad—yes, you can support the Shia militia but you can't give support to the Kurds—for whatever reason, the weapons dribble in and this is wrong. This is immoral.

The other point I would make, I just wanted to ask you some questions on the issue of the sale of female captives from religious minority groups to ISIS fighters. How extensively has ISIS been involved in what we here call sex trafficking or slavery, frankly, particularly the kidnapping and sale of women and girls from these overrun communities? Has it been an outcome of lawlessness or is it part of a more deliberate ISIS policy to destroy and to subjugate those who do not share their fanaticism? Ms. Isaac.

Ms. ISAAC. Looking at the ISIS philosophy, they believe that the Yazidi people in particular are not only to be tortured but they are to be destroyed in every single way possible. They want them off the face of this earth. And so it is a philosophy to destroy them and to torture them.

With the girls particularly that I met, they in one night, because they felt safe in the beginning in Sinjar town, and in one night ISIS came and took all of these girls. And they told them first, they gave them an option. They said will you become a Muslim? Will you convert to Islam? And many of them said no. And they told them, you are going to be Muslim regardless because we are going to sleep with you. And the moment that we do that, once we rape you, you will be Muslim.

Many of these girls who chose not to be, some were raped and came back believing that they were forced into this religion. This is barbaric. It is systematic. Today it starts with the Yazidis. Tomorrow it is going to be not only the Christians but every woman that doesn't fit within their philosophy. We need to stop the menace that is going on there. We need to stop it at its root.

This is a nerve center. Right now all the crazies from all over the world are coming to this center point, to this nerve center. If we can cut the snake at its head we can diffuse them. Their sex trafficking is systematic and it will continue, and it can reach our families if we don't do something about it. Thank you.

Chairman ROYCE. Let me also ask about psychological counseling, and I would ask that of the panel. What type of trauma resources are available right now for those who have escaped and what more is needed? Sister?

Sister MOMEKA. Yes. I would say from my work on the ground we don't have that strong programs to talk about trauma. Because I just experienced a case about 4 weeks ago, a woman who was released by ISIS with 20 Yazidi women. The Yazidi women told us that this is a Christian, you take her and we go to our Yazidi families.

So the woman was totally devastated. She is in her 40s. She was brutally beaten, raped constantly, yet that her psychological situation is totally destroyed that she can't control herself anymore. When she tells her story how they tortured her in so many ways that when one of the sisters who took her and took care of her, she found all her body was so many cigarettes with the burn of the smoke and all that.

So the woman now, we put her in a safer place, yet we are trying to find a good psychological treatment for her yet it is not that available where we live exactly. So we lack for that thing. So the social psychological programs, I think they are the most important thing to look forward to work on at this moment.

Chairman ROYCE. Well, thank you. My time is about to expire so I will go to Mr. Engel.

Mr. ENGEL. Thank you, Mr. Chairman. Dr. Hanson, let me start with you. First of all, thank you for being here today and thank you for your work to help Iraqi citizens save their religious history. As you know, America has a long history of leading the world in efforts to protect religious and cultural sites from destruction and you are carrying this legacy forward today.

During times of crisis such as those in Iraq and Syria, our first priority must always be in saving lives. And I thank the other witnesses in emphasizing that as well—Ms. Isaac about the women's aspect and our witnesses about how this is affecting everybody. We are committed to the priority of saving lives, but we also must ensure that we stop ISIS from destroying the history of these groups. And as we create safe havens to protect religious minorities, Dr. Hanson, how do we also keep the religious sites and cultural history safe from ISIS as well?

Ms. HANSON. Thank you. I think it is very important that we make sure that we are supporting local actions; that local actors are able to protect the sites. It is much like with the firemen that you make sure that you provide the hose and the water. I also think that in terms of safe havens for individuals, we can also think about that as safe havens within a country for portable objects and artifacts and that there are safe locations where things can be moved. And we have seen that successfully take place in Mali, for instance, recently.

Mr. ENGEL. Thank you. Ms. Kabawat, let me ask you this question. According to State Department testimony last summer, some of ISIS's religious minority captives have been able to escape while their captors were distracted by coalition air strikes. To what extent have coalition air strikes affected religious minorities?

Ms. KABAWAT. When we talk about effect of the air strikes it affect both the majority and the minorities, because they did hit some civilian places. And I was in Harem 1 month before they started and where I was, was lots of civilians has been hit. And the problem is that they need to have more homework. They should know where is the civilians. So when we want to say targeting civilians, minorities, we need to say targeting civilians and we cannot say only minority because sometimes it is hitting everybody. Thank you.

Mr. ENGEL. Thank you. Let me ask Ms. Isaac and also Sister. ISIS is raging obviously a campaign of destruction against religious sites across the territory that they control. We saw the slides and pictures. Can you comment on the impact the destruction of religious sites has on the people who share a religious connection to those sites? What do we lose when ISIS destroys these sites? Why don't we start with Sister and then Ms. Isaac.

Sister MOMEKA. What do we lose? I would say we lost everything, sir. We lost everything that today every Christian that is living in the region of Kurdistan we feel we don't have dignity anymore. When you lose your home you lose everything you have. You lose your heritage, your culture. You become with no identity. And today that is how we see ourselves.

And the most brutal thing was to us when it was put on TV that two monasteries that were one of them bombed and another one destroyed just was a sign for us and that your history is gone, you are nothing anymore. That is how we see ourselves now, homeless.

Mr. ENGEL. Thank you. Ms. Isaac?

Ms. ISAAC. Thank you, Member Engel. As an American of Egyptian descent I moved to Egypt when I was 13. And I remember holding on to the heritage knowing that there were ancient churches still there. Even if we were the minority, I had a tie. I could identify with my ancient churches.

Today in Iraq you have the Lalish Center which is still preserved with the Yazidis. That is the mecca for them. That is their Rome. Today they hold on to that. And the Peshmerga army is working so hard to protect that area because they know that if that is gone the Yazidi people will feel hopeless. They won't be able to identify anymore with the land that they have remained in for many, many years.

For religious minorities in this region our heritage is everything. It ties us to that land. It keeps us there. And we are not supposed to just be there to survive, we should be living there to thrive. We should be able to worship freely, go to the heritage sites, bring our children and our grandchildren and talk about that history. Without those sites we have lost it all. Thank you.

Mr. ENGEL. Thank you. And let me again thank all four of you for wonderful testimony and for wonderful coverage. We really appreciate it. Thank you, Mr. Chairman.

Chairman ROYCE. Thank you. Our Chairman Emeritus Ileana Ros-Lehtinen.

Ms. ROS-LEHTINEN. Thank you so much, Mr. Chairman. Today's hearing as we know focuses on a subject that all too often gets overlooked or ignored when discussing the crisis in the Middle East, and specifically the fight against ISIL. We have discussed this in our Middle East and North Africa Subcommittee on several occasions alongside Chairman Smith and his subcommittee, and Chris Smith has been a tireless advocate for this issue.

ISIL has issued warnings to Christians in Iraq that they can convert, pay taxes or be killed. Churches are being destroyed, religious artifact sites are being raided, and many Christians and other religious minorities have been forced to flee. ISIL massacred 20 Coptic Christians in cold blood in Egypt, but the list goes on and on. However, we must acknowledge that ISIL doesn't just target religious minorities. Everyone who doesn't ascribe to its form of Islam is a target.

So that is why it is imperative that we not only defeat ISIL but we find a way to defeat its radical ideology as well. It is also important to recognize that the persecution of religious minorities isn't just isolated to ISIL or to Iraq or to Syria. The U.S. Commission on International Religious Freedom has repeatedly called upon the Obama administration to designate countries like Iraq, Syria and Egypt as Countries of Particular Concern. That is a special classification. Why? For their systematic, ongoing and egregious abuses that the religious minorities face in those countries.

Many of us in this committee have decried the fact that the Iranian regime's deplorable human rights record and its persecution of religious minorities were not made a part of the nuclear negotiations from day one since the P5+1 efforts were announced. A nuclear deal will legitimize the Iranian regime and will only serve to make the atmosphere even worse for religious minorities in Iran.

Iran's meddling in Iraq, its support for Shiite militias, those have played a significant role in the rise of ISIL and the current difficulties that we face in the region in the fight against the terror group in Iraq and Syria. And now we have seen the size of the religious minority communities decline dramatically in Iraq and Syria as a result of ISIL's onslaught.

So Sister Diana, I will ask you. You have felt the pain and the suffering in your own community and you have been witness to what ISIL has done to ancient religious communities of Iraq. You have been displaced twice. Can you describe for us the conditions in Mosul where you were forced to flee to Kurdistan, and could you also please detail the conditions in Kurdistan? And lastly, what more can we do to meet the needs of religious minority communities? Where can we be most effective?

Sister MOMEKA. Thank you, Ms. Ros. I would answer your question in a story that touches my heart a lot and the heart of the people that we are working with. When we were forced to leave our children became without any education, without school. So as a congregation we care a lot about education as Dominicans, so we start opening kindergartens. So we had 135 in one of the kindergartens. In one of their classes we handed them papers to draw on the paper. Amazingly, most of the children, they draw back home, their hometowns. They draw, some, their beds, church, homes, everything that they relate back home. So when we ask them, why did you do that? They said, like, we miss home. We want to go back home. We want to live normal life.

A 5-year-old, when he stood up and he said, I don't feel like I am home here. When I was home I used to go to the kindergarten. I used to go to church with my family. I used to play with my toys, with my friends. That was a normal life when we were back in our homes. We used to live normal life. We would have education. Our parents, brothers, sisters, if they are employed they would go to work.

Now it is the opposite. People are jobless. Women do not have any work to do. They are living in containers or living in unfinished buildings facing terrible conditions besides. The humanitarian aid is not enough for them. So it is so different that today even our children, what I want to say, our children, they feel that they don't have a place to live properly. They don't have home. So our life has changed tremendously. And since before we were this bridge that we can connect among the diversities, now we feel we are alone. We are abandoned. That is how we feel.

Ms. ROS-LEHTINEN. Thank you very much, Mr. Chairman. We certainly know that ISIL doesn't discriminate. You are either with the terrorists or they will destroy you or subjugate you. Thank you.

Chairman ROYCE. Thank you, Ileana. We will go to Mr. Brad Sherman from California.

Mr. SHERMAN. Mr. Chairman, the two most powerful forces in the Syria-Iraq-Lebanon area are the Shiite alliance in Iran on the one hand, and the extremists Sunnis on the other. What we have seen our friends, Saudi Arabia and others, do, is move toward what they will accept as ''moderate Islam or acceptable Islam,'' and embrace the Brotherhood—Turkey, Qatar—and perhaps even al-Nustra, which is after all part of al-Qaeda. Had we done more to strengthen the more reasonable Sunnis earlier in the process, perhaps Saudi Arabia would not be taking that action. The good news is there has been reports in the last ½ hour that the number two commander in ISIS has been killed. I hope that is true. We will see.

Mr. Chairman, you commented that ISIS has all this Iraqi currency. Iraq should of course issue new currency making its own currency invalid. Many countries have done this. This is a process that is hated by corrupt politicians and drug dealers with large amounts of currency of their own, and of course the Iraqi Government has failed to do so which leads to a possible conclusion that perhaps corrupt politicians with huge stashes of cash have some power in Baghdad.

This Congress passed the Near East South Central Asia Religious Freedom Act. That required that the State Department have a special envoy for religious minorities in that region. We are still waiting for someone to be appointed. Do not hold your breath. The attitude of the administration toward following laws just because they are laws is less than I think it ought to be.

Speaking of laws passed by Congress, we authorized $1.6 billion in NDAA to counter ISIL. This included, the authorization was amended to include provisions for local security forces on the Nineveh Plain including Assyrian and Yazidi forces. So far that hasn't happened. And of course communities that cannot defend themselves are in a difficult circumstance on the Nineveh Plain.

One of our witnesses has been unabashed in support of the Kurdish Government. Ms. Isaac. I had in my office yesterday representatives of the Yazidi, Assyrian and Kurdish communities that took a very different view of the Kurdish Government. Perhaps a balance between the two is that the Kurdish Government has provided sanctuary but has not allowed these groups to form their own national guard battalions. And no group on the Nineveh Plain is going to be safe unless they have their own national guard.

Mr. Chairman, I would like to see us bring to testify before this committee one of the Yazidi women who has successfully fled from ISIS. This would require that the State Department provide an entry visa, and if the woman or girl was coming from Kurdish areas we would need to get an exit visa from that government. Mr. Chairman?

Chairman ROYCE. Just if I could interrupt for a minute. We did have a young Yazidi woman, a young girl, slated to testify. She had to drop off of the trip because of health reasons. But we will achieve your goal here. And I will relinquish the time back to you.

Mr. SHERMAN. Thank you. Ms. Kabawat, minorities are being given the choice—convert, flee, die or pay a very unfair tax. Now I put three of those in one category. The jizya is something that Muslim governments have imposed upon the minority communities for centuries, and in prior centuries it has been a tax that was endurable. Of course it is outrageous and unfair.

Is ISIS imposing a tax that is outrageous, unfair, but is a practical thing that the communities could pay, or is it just an excuse for them to say, well, we want to confiscate everything on Monday. That is your Monday tax. And on Tuesday you don't have anything left so we are going to kill you. Is ISIS offering to allow at least Christians—the Yazidis of course would be treated differently under their rules—a chance to stay in their homes and pay a tax consistent with what is possible? Of course it is outrageous.

Ms. KABAWAT. Just talking about Syria, in Raqqa where the ISIS has full control most of the Christian get out. There is not many Christians now in the ISIS-controlled area like Menbij or Raqqa. The one that are there they in hiding. They did say that they are asking for jizya and it happened few times, but I think there is not many Christians in this area. They are already gone. And in other things, the Christians now they are all in Aleppo or stayed in Idlib, and others they have been away. But where there has been now in where there is the moderate Muslims' control, they are not being asked for any jizya because they treat them as an equal citizen. Thank you.

Mr. SHERMAN. I believe my time is expired.

Chairman ROYCE. Thank you, Mr. Sherman. Mr. Dana Rohrabacher of California.

Mr. ROHRABACHER. Thank you very much. Let me identify myself with Mr. Sherman's point about the Iraqi currency. We must get to the bottom of who the heck is paying for ISIS, what government is responsible for providing them money, and whoever that is we need to make sure we come down like a ton of bricks on that government. And we must make sure that that is a high priority for this government to find out who is financing this sinful and this horrendous atrocity against the people of the world. Whatever faith you are, whether you are Islam or Christian or whatever faith you are, this is an abomination to any belief in God, and we must stand in unity with people of all faiths in this endeavor.

And I want to thank Chairman Royce and Engel who have demonstrated again the bipartisan nature of many of these challenges that we face and that standing together America, if nothing else, because we come from, we are made up of every race, religion and ethnic group in the world. We are supposed to be the one that sets the standard for the world. And we can do that by making sure that we don't cozy up to people and remain friends with people who are financing this type of atrocity.

And I would like to—look, it is a perplexing position because people are being murdered in this part of the world. Your friends, your relatives, really innocent human beings are being savaged. Should our focus be on trying to defeat and eliminate the evil forces that are at play or should it be to extract people from this danger zone to get them here? I wonder if any of you have any thoughts on that. All of you, just go right ahead.

Ms. KABAWAT. Mr. Congressman, I think the solution is to stop the conflict. We have a conflict in Middle East. I am talking now about Syria. We have a conflict, and you are asking about who is paying ISIS. They don't—they took banks, they steal, they do everything they can not to have to be dependent on anybody to get their money. If we want to get rid of them we need to end the conflicts. There is a conflicts now in Syria and people are suffering, and today we need to think about those civilians, how to stop their suffering.

There are ISIS attacks every day. People are scared. And I know many people there escaped. Even if they are Muslims they escape because ISIS will be threaten their lives. So if we want to stop the ISIS we need to stop the conflict in Syria. We need to stop the caliphate and we need to stop the dictator. Most of them are the enemies of the security and the safety and the future for Syria. Thank you.

Ms. ISAAC. Congressman Rohrabacher, when I take a look at all the religious minorities that I have met when I was in Iraq and I look at their ancient history, you know that they belong there and they want to stay there. And if we try to get rid of the problem by just bringing the religious minorities here——

Mr. ROHRABACHER. Yes.

Ms. ISAAC [continuing]. ISIS will spread everywhere. It will continue. Right now we have a diverse fabric in the Middle East and it is really protecting not only the region but the entire world. The fact that there are Christians and Yazidis and Jews in that region today makes the Middle East what it is. We need to look at the bigger fight and understand that ISIS is against the entire world. Their short term plan right now is trying to get rid of the religious minorities of the region and creating their state. But tomorrow it is going to be to attack the entire world.

Mr. ROHRABACHER. I think that your point is well made. And I just, I know that Sister Diana had trouble even getting here. We should not be having barriers to people especially coming here to make their case and to warn us. At the same time, and I have just a few seconds left, let me just say that we need also to make sure that we are standing behind those people like our friends the Kurds up in Erbil who are making this stand. We haven't even solved that problem yet, Mr. Chairman, where our supplies could go directly to the Kurds. Some of them are now, but as many of them you have to go through Baghdad in order to get the supplies there.

We should be making sure anyone in that region who is fighting ISIS gets the full support and direct support from the people of the United States. And you are in our thoughts and prayers. We know that you are all these communities. I visited a community in Syria. My wife and I actually went and said that was one of our most important experiences in our life where we said the Lord's Prayer in Aramaic as Jesus spoke. So hang tough, we are with you.

Chairman ROYCE. Brian Higgins of New York.

Mr. HIGGINS. Thank you, Mr. Chairman. And I just want to thank the panel here. Testimony has been both eloquent and compelling. I just want to focus for a moment on the Christian community in the Middle East. ISIS has declared war on Christians. ISIS wants genocide now. They want to eradicate Christians from the Middle East and Africa. Christian kids have been beheaded, their mothers raped and their fathers crucified, literally.

ISIS believes that Christians are standing in the way of their world conquest. Anything that is pre-Islamic they want to destroy and want to prepare the world for the coming of the Islamic Caliphate. Christians in the Middle East and Africa are losing entire communities that have lived peacefully for 2,000 years. Five hundred thousand Christians, Christian Arabs, have been driven out of Syria during the last 3 years of civil war. Christians have been persecuted and killed from Lebanon to Sudan, well, now South Sudan, and civil wars have lasted decades.

In Iraq, Mosul is a Christian city, the second largest city in Iraq. Christians have been living there for 1,700 years as you know better than anybody. After the fall of Saddam, the numbers of Christians in Iraq were estimated to be about 45,000. Sister, today how many Christians are living in Mosul?

Sister MOMEKA. Very few. Only those who have been held hostages there. We don't have the exact number. Maybe a couple hundred or less.

Mr. HIGGINS. 100 or less. And most of those who have fled have moved up to Kurdistan?

Sister MOMEKA. First of all, they fled to my hometown which is called Qaraqosh, and where we——

Mr. HIGGINS. Which is where?

Sister MOMEKA. It is called Qaraqosh.

Mr. HIGGINS. Which is?

Sister MOMEKA. Which is close to Mosul, about 20 minutes distance southwest of Mosul.

Mr. HIGGINS. West?

Sister MOMEKA. Yes. And after a week or so our displacement happened, which would have never thought that would happen with the couple hours that we were forced to leave, which take, it is about 1 hour distance from my hometown to Kurdistan. It took us 11 hours to go there because some were marching, some were driving, and because it was a traumatic state for us. So I would say like very few Christians have stayed in Mosul or that they couldn't leave because they were asleep when that happened.

Mr. HIGGINS. Is it the hope of the Christians from Mosul who have been forced to flee to one day return?

Sister MOMEKA. Yes. The message that I was given before I left, they said to me—I have been working every day with the IDPs. That is what they call us, actually, there. They said to me, Sister, just please tell the community, tell the Members of the Congress that help us to go back home. We want to go back home.

Mr. HIGGINS. What has been the position of Prime Minister Abadi relative to the Christian community of Iraq?

You don't need to say. I get it. Yes. And this is, we were told after Nouri al-Malikim who was a thug, left, that things would change. That the new Iraqi Government would be inclusive of all minorities and communities. And political stability is dependent on the ability to embrace the Kurds, the Shia, the Sunni, but also the Christian community of Iraq. So that is not happening, clearly, and this is just one of many consequences of the failure to embrace the minority community.

And this is again the larger problem in the Middle East. It is a highly, highly pluralistic part of the world, and unless and until you have minority rights you will never have peace and stability. Because a guy like Bashar al-Assad is clearly a bad guy. But what is happening is minority groups have a tendency to gravitate to him for one reason, because if the majority Sunni become head of that country all the minorities will be slaughtered. So long as there is a zero sum game in the Middle East, the sum will always be zero.

And I often say in game theory there is also what is referred to as a variable sum game saying that there can be many winners. And whatever we do there, however much humanitarian aid we provide there, however much military support we provide in the Middle East, internally the leadership that we get behind, the United States, the leadership that we support have to embrace, they have an obligation to embrace the minority community. Because we will be sitting here 5 years from now, 10 years from now, 20 years from now and we will be having the same discussion with no progress whatsoever.

So again thank you very much for your testimony and I will yield back.

Chairman ROYCE. We go now to Mr. Chris Smith of New Jersey.

Mr. SMITH OF NEW JERSEY. Thank you very much, Mr. Chairman, and thank you for calling this very, very important hearing and to our very distinguished witnesses for your courage, for so effectively articulating the plight of the suffering minorities in the Middle East, particularly Christians, so thank you for that. And all those who are suffering at the hands of ISIS and people who are extremists.

I would like to ask just a couple of questions. The United Nations High Commissioner for Human Rights pointed out that the ISIS violence against Christians and other religious minorities ''may constitute genocide.'' May? I find it extraordinary. The Genocide Convention couldn't be clearer eliminating in whole or in part, even the threat rises to the level of being genocide.

And of course the international community has always been slow to recognize genocide. We didn't do it with Srebrenica, we didn't do it in—when I say ''we'' I mean the international community—when it came to Sudan. And 100 years later, we still, only 24 or so countries have recognized the Armenian genocide. So we seem to gag on the word, and I have tried to get administration witnesses to say that what is happening to the Christians rises to the level of genocide and that simply is not stated.

Chairman Emeritus Ileana Ros-Lehtinen and I have chaired a number of hearings on the genocide. We had one last year, genocidal attacks against Christians and other religious minorities in Syria and Iraq, and again we keep getting, well, we will look into it, we will get back. But just say it and say it clearly and unambiguously. And I have chaired 14 hearings on the suffering of Christians, particularly in the Middle East, and we are still getting a lack of embrace of the magnitude and the hostility toward people of the Christian faith.

I would point out that sometimes past is prologue. The Clinton administration opposed the International Religious Freedom Act of 1998. I know because I held all the hearings and marked up the bill. He ended up signing it, but then now we find under this administration the post of Ambassador-at-Large was idle, was left vacant for half of this Presidency. We have a very good man now in that position, David Saperstein, Rabbi Saperstein who is trying to make up, I think, for lost time. But it was a revelation of priorities that we did not have a person sitting in that very important position.

Approximately 7 months ago legislation passed, totally bipartisan, to establish a Special Envoy to Promote Religious Freedom of Religious Minorities in the Near East and South Central Asia. It was no secret the administration didn't want it, but he did sign it. The President did sign it into law when it passed in a bipartisan way. But now for 7 months nobody has been selected to take that position. That person should have the ear of the President and could shuttle back and forth and assess what is going on on the ground with clarity and to speak out boldly. Nobody has that position. I find that appalling. And you might want to comment on that as well.

And finally, let me ask you. The faith of the young people has to have been—I know we saw that wonderful video of the resiliency of those young women, but the faith of the young people has to be shattered. They must wonder where are the faithful elsewhere particularly in the United States. I don't think we have done enough, again the special envoy vacancy speaks volumes to that. But if I could ask you, where is the faith of these young people?

Sister MOMEKA. As a matter of fact, Mr. Smith, is that our faith, it is amazingly that we see it is increasing more and more. It is making us more stronger. We left churches that were like used to be filled with people. Now we have only one church and you see like young people, or all people they see that we still have faith in God; that we were displaced yet we feel that the hand of God is still with us.

So in the midst of, as my colleagues said, in the midst of this darkness of this suffering we see a God that is holding us. He is holding us, otherwise we wouldn't have been able to be witnessing to our faith that is increasing day after day. And I think this is one of the gifts of the Holy Spirit that is giving us the strength to continue our faith and to be strong to stay in our country. Some left, yes, but they are willing to go back when we go back home. And we have this hope somebody we will go back home, and that will come through your help.

Ms. KABAWAT. Mr. Congressman, the faith with the Christian community in Damascus is increasing. We are Christian for 2,000 years. My family were Christian for the last 2,000 years. Today we are more involved in a humanitarian war. We know we have to lead by example. This is our Christianity, to help others. That is why my family today still in Damascus. My immediate family in Damascus, but their faith is to distribute bread for the poor, to take care of others because this is what Jesus Christ told us, to take care of the small people.

So in Aleppo, churches are open to like hospitals. In Idlib, when they liberated Idlib, the Christian there work with the Muslim in the humanitarian issues. So yes, we are Christians, but today more than ever we are Christians because we know that we need to practice our Christianity on the ground and to take care of the small people who are suffering.

Ms. ISAAC. Congressman Smith, I went to Egypt and I met the families, 15 of the 21 families that had victims that were slaughtered in Libya. I was astonished by their faith. As a fellow Christian I thought how would I be if I was the situation today? Meeting the fathers that said to me, thank God that today they are in heaven. Thank God. A wife talking to me about how her husband had said, I am going to Libya and I will be in danger. But if I don't make it, teach my children. Teach them the principles of Jesus Christ.

That is the story. These are the accounts of their faith. And I have seen it in Iraq across the board how Christians are standing strong and helping all, helping the Yazidis. In fact we had a case. I remember there was a group of Yazidis that found a local church and that church was providing care for them, providing a home for them. This is what they are doing. They are struggling, but they are giving everything that they have. So thank you.

Chairman ROYCE. We go to Mr. William Keating of Massachusetts.

Mr. KEATING. Thank you, Mr. Chairman, for holding this hearing, and thank you as witnesses. And I want to let you know we all share your commitment to saving lives, saving religious and cultural heritages and artifacts and stopping human trafficking. I also want to acknowledge, as Dr. Hanson has, the legislation of Chairman Royce, Ranking Member Engel, Mr. Smith, who I am proud to join in working on this area.

But I want to focus on one thing I believe that we can do more of in the U.S. to really stop these terrible actions by ISIL, and that is to look at an issue that time and time again has come to my attention as ranking member on the Terrorism, Trade, and Nonproliferation Subcommittee, in this committee as well as counterterrorism and homeland security, and that is the issue where ISIL is not only destroying cultural and religious heritages, particularly in Iraq and Syria, but it is doubling down on that activity. And either through taxing criminals or themselves they are trafficking in these looted antiquities and financing their own terrorist operations again, so it becomes cyclical. And I saw firsthand, I just came back days ago visiting eight countries in the Mideast and Europe, just how this is occurring, and in fact had comments from the leaders in these areas how smuggling in these antiquities is such a force of financing for these terrorists.

So what I am doing today as well is introducing legislation to prevent trafficking in Cultural Property Act, is the name of the legislation, and it is geared in on one aspect that I think we could easily move toward these activities. And that is the fact that even the agencies themselves in Customs and Border Patrol and in ICE, they are saying that they are not as coordinated as they should be. They don't have the tools to gear in on this when these artifacts and trafficking, when this trafficking comes through our own border in the U.S.

One of the things we have to do, I believe, and that is what this legislation does, is to work to make sure there is principal leadership there, a designated person to really key in on this. And also, importantly, to have the training in this activity. Because even if that commitment and coordination is there, it is important that these U.S. officials receive sufficient training in identifying cultural property from regions that the greatest risk of looting, like Iraq and Syria, and that they know the techniques specifically related to this so they can investigate and prosecute this kind of activity to really quell the demand in unfortunately one of the destination areas of the world, the United States of America.

So we are working on that. I would like your opinion of how from your perspective this could be helpful as well, and I think particularly Dr. Hanson has some experience in that regard.

Ms. HANSON. Thank you. What you mentioned is incredibly important and it is vital that we remove the financial incentive for terrorist groups like ISIS to loot cultural sites, religious sites. One of the things we have noticed is that prior to the demolition of religious sites, particularly shrines, Yazidi shrines and tombs, ISIS has gone in in advance and looted artifacts out of that area. Architectural elements, things that they can sell.

And the reason why they are doing looting in those instances, and also in the images we saw of Dura-Europos, is that there is a market for it. And your legislation and what you mentioned is incredibly important in taking action to reduce that market. Right now it is crucial that we get import restrictions on stolen material from Syria put into place in the U.S. As a market country, our demand for that in the U.S. is some of what fuels ISIS's actions.

Mr. KEATING. Yes, I was really intrigued when ISIS will show the videos of their desecrating these religious institutions and sending those videos to the world and saying they are doing it because of the sense of pureness, and that their only, their narrow, if you want to even call it religious beliefs should be the only beliefs. Yet, if these artifacts that they are destroying so no one else will be able to culturally go forth in heritage, if they are portable, then moving them around and profiting on them and preserving them just to fuel their own terrorism which, I think, shows where their priorities are.

Quickly, could you just tell me the scope of this? I heard in my recent visit it is in the tens of millions of dollars that they are getting from this, and that is, I think, under reporting because it is pretty hard to get a figure on it. Just quickly, last question.

Ms. HANSON. Very difficult to get a dollar amount on it. We know that it is significant. As you saw with Dora-Europos, those are moonscapes now and all of those artifacts that come out of the ground can get financial benefits for them. So you just have to assume that even the lowest estimates have to be staggering. I can't give you an exact dollar amount, and that is something that we are continuing to research and work on.

Mr. KEATING. Yes. I heard 37 million. I yield back, Mr. Chairman.

Chairman ROYCE. Mr. Scott Perry of Pennsylvania.

Mr. PERRY. Thank you, Mr. Chairman. Ladies, I appreciate you being here. The stories are shocking to our conscience. Americans need to have their conscience unfortunately continued to be shocked because of what continues to happen. But the stories break our hearts. There is not much else to say than that.

Dr. Hanson, we have seen ISIS crucify in public squares, stone to death women, throw gay people off of buildings, then they proudly tweet, post these horrific acts on YouTube, other social media. In fact, they have gained followers based on the use of social media. The question is, has ISIS's propaganda campaign affected the disposition of religious minority communities beyond Iraq and Syria, and what effective action would you recommend the United States take to combat ISIS, the propaganda, and especially on social media? Have you researched that and what your recommendations?

Ms. HANSON. My research doesn't directly encompass social media. One of the things that we have noticed in working with the cultural heritage destruction and the religious heritage destruction is that the videos are very clearly designed to demonstrate power and demonstrate terror.

Right now we have an NSF grant to study what is happening with the phenomenon of damage to cultural heritage and why it is occurring, and we are working on answering some very basic questions like when does cultural heritage damage take place? Is it before or after the religious minority population is physically threatened and murdered? When it comes to social media what is happening with videos is exactly the same thing that is happening with the videos of deaths and destructions. The cultural heritage sites are being destroyed in a way to demonstrate power and terror.

Mr. PERRY. We will wait to hear back from you based on the ground if you have any recommendations.

I would like to turn to Ms. Kabawat; is that right? We have been told by the administration that the U.S. Government is examining all, and I emphasize all, viable options for protecting minority vulnerable communities and halting the parade of atrocities ISIS is committing. What do you view? I mean you have lived it on the ground. What do you view as the viable options for the U.S. to protect these communities if there are any?

Ms. KABAWAT. Again, Mr. Congressman, I feel on the ground when they hear this kind of comment the people get little bit disappointed and angry. We can't protect one minorities without thinking about what is happening to the whole country. We are talking about thousands of refugees, of Christians, but also there are millions of Sunnis and they are paying the price from ISIS.

So the solution will be a package. We don't want to be isolated from the other Syrian who we have been raised and lived with them all our lives. I want a solution not only for the minorities, I want a solution for whole Syria. We need to stop the conflict. So when we say we want to protect us it is offending me, because I don't want to be protected when my other neighbors who is Sunnis is being under attack. So please protect the whole civilian. We have so many moderate Muslim, Christians. We live together all our lives. So if you want to protect us as a Christian, I am asking you, protect also my neighbors. Thank you.

Mr. PERRY. Sister Diana, do you think that the ISIS targeting of minority communities in areas has primarily been due to strategic opportunity just because you are there and it is easy, you are vulnerable? Or is there something more deliberate? I mean would you articulate if it is one or the other or a combination of the two?

Sister MOMEKA. As I mentioned earlier, Mr. Congressman, that it was quite shock for us because we used to watch the news on TV that ISIS took over Mosul, but we never thought some day in a few hours we will be out of our homes left with nothing at all. I myself only with my habit and my purse, which I was lucky I had my passport in it. Most of my sisters and most people left with no documents, nothing.

So it start with Nineveh Plain and it was gradually, so if it was deliberately or not I can't say that. But all what I know now, we were driven out of our homes within couple hours. That was it. Without any warning.

Mr. PERRY. My time is expired. Thank you.

Chairman ROYCE. We go now to Mr. David Cicilline of Rhode Island.

Mr. CICILLINE. Thank you, Mr. Chairman, and thank you for calling this hearing. Thank you to our witnesses for your really courageous testimony, and the description of the horrors and the violence and the sadistic behavior of this terrorist organization I hope is something that the whole world understands better as a result of your being here today at significant personal risk to yourselves and the work that you are doing. So thank you for being here.

As my colleague from Massachusetts said, I think our whole committee is of course committed to doing everything that we can to support the preservation of cultural and religious sites, but more importantly, in my view, to do all that we can to protect and save lives. And this effort to destroy cultural and religious sites, I think, is clearly an extension of this terrorist effort to eliminate entire religious communities in this region and something we have to respond to in the strongest terms.

So my first question is, I know there are religious minorities—Christians, Yazidis, Shabaks—that have faced terrible persecution and have fled their ancient homelands, but they are unable to cross the border in many instances so they are not technically refugees, they are internally displaced persons. And these are obviously very vulnerable populations. What can we do, what can the United States be doing better to help these communities that are trapped in very unsafe locations be in a safer place and provide some protection, these internally displaced what I would call refugees even though they are not technically refugees because they haven't left the borders of their own country? Anyone?

Ms. ISAAC. Mr. Congressman, when I went to northern Iraq and I met the Kurdistan Regional Government I was amazed at the work that they have done. Not because of meetings I went to but because of the ground. I went and saw the girls that were kidnapped and raped by ISIS, for example, and I saw the care that they were getting.

Yes, the Kurdistan Regional Government does not have a lot of resources, but they are still doing everything that they can to make Yazidis, like the girls that we met, Christians, and all other religious minorities feel like an equal. In fact, a lot of these workers have been unpaid for months at a time to give everything that they have to these religious minorities to show that they truly are a safe haven. I have never seen a people like the Kurdish people, because they have gone through their own atrocities so many times they understand what it is like to be a religious minority fleeing.

So I say the solution is to support, number one, the Peshmerga army who is really the ones on the front lines and are the boots on the ground. Let us help them as they fight this war. Let us support them in any way they can. Let us help the Kurdistan Regional Government by providing more humanitarian assistance to help with not just the medical care but also the psychological care.

When I was in Jordan helping the Syrian refugees, I remember there was this little boy, and U.N. Secretary General Ban Ki-Moon had flown over, and he said to me, do you see that helicopter over there? I said yes. He goes, I hope to God it bombs Jordan. I was shocked. I said why would you say something like that? He said, because it happened to me, it has to happen to everyone else.

A lot of the children that are coming in to these territories have seen so much destruction and trauma and they don't know how to deal with it, so in order to protect this worlds we need to focus on this new generation. And how do we do that? By supporting the Kurdistan Regional Government as they work on not just the medical care but that psychological element as well. And of course to support the partners like Egypt and Jordan who are also bringing in refugees and taking care of their people. In Egypt alone they are educating 14,000 college students from Syria, and thousands, about 40,000 students in elementary schools are being taken care of. So let us support them on the ground.

Mr. CICILLINE. I was just in Jordan and saw at the border, the Syrian border, the incredible work of the Jordanians supporting over 1½ million refugees fleeing Syria, and we have to be sure that we continue to support that.

Ms. Kabawat, I know you have——

Ms. KABAWAT. Again, Mr. Congressman, I really emphasize about the solution of the protected zone. We need it. I have been also in Jordan last month. It is so important to start thinking about this. We need to get the civilian in a safe way, in a safe area they can be protected from the ISIS and from the barrel bombs of the Syrian regimes. We need it. And this will give better position for Turkey and Jordan so they can take care of other things.

And we really thanks to the American for all the humanitarian aids they are giving to the Syrian people. We appreciate it. We know that you are doing a lot. But they really need to be in a safe zone, so I really asking you and seeking this. It is so important. Thank you.

Mr. CICILLINE. Mr. Chairman, if I might just ask indulgence for one final question. I just want to pick up on Congressman Higgins' questions about the role of the current Iraqi Government. There are many people who argue that ISIS is an outgrowth of policies from Iraqi and Syrian Governments that have marginalized Sunnis in particular. What do we need to see from the current Iraqi Government or a future Syrian Government to demonstrate the kind of tolerance and inclusiveness that will prevent this kind of violence, and should the United States be doing more to condition some of our support to the Iraqi Government on their commitment to take certain steps to protect minority populations and build a more inclusive government? I mean that is, the Syrian solution is the long-term answer, but in this interim period can we be doing more to demand more of the current Iraqi Government?

Sister MOMEKA. Mr. Congressman, I think it is very important to do such things. Previous, I mean to your question, I mean as we are known as IDPs we will be like that forever if we don't return home. So if there is efforts from both parts to help us to return home, I think that will be the solution, of course with your help. So that will give us a better life, otherwise there will be no education.

And it is not about the education and health care because that won't happen when you are an IDP. You don't have an identity or any entity there. Our entity is back where we belong. So I think if there are efforts from both parts to return home, there where we can start rebuild, there where we can start all over again. Thank you.

Ms. KABAWAT. Regarding Syria, and you are talking about long-term, we need to think about few things. First, we need a transitions not to destroy the institutions, and this will happen only if we have a political solution. We need to pressure the regime to come to the negotiation table and make a, we need a transitions and we need to include everybody, and everything will be good if we can end it within a political solutions. This is a long term and this is the best way to protect minorities, to save the institutions and have a transitions government include everybody.

Mr. CICILLINE. Thank you very much. Thank you, Mr. Chairman.

Chairman ROYCE. Ms. Kabawat, if I could interject here. You are suggesting that to get there you need a no-fly zone, a safe zone over Aleppo and the other areas where, in Aleppo, for example, the business community, the Sunni and Christian and Alawite business community is trying to hold out there but they have ISIS on the front line, but then intermittently the barrel bombs and the chemical attacks occur from the Assad regime which are dropped on the city that is trying to hold out against ISIS. And so you are saying you believe if there was a no-fly zone and there was a prohibition from the dropping of the barrel bombs that would help civil society take a foothold there? And could you explain that thinking to me?

Ms. KABAWAT. I did witness the barrel bombs when I was in Aleppo, and it is very, very hard for the civil society to grow when there is an immediate threat to your lives. Yes, I am not a military expert, but I believe that we need to stop the barrel bombs. This is a first step for the community, for everybody.

Chairman ROYCE. And you think also that in doing that it helps drive an impetus for a settlement because then they can see that the society can't be overrun there.

Ms. KABAWAT. Exactly. And we did. There is so many example before from the local councils that they could run the community and they can include the Christians, believe me.

Chairman ROYCE. Well, I have noticed. I mean the battalions, I have seen Christian female battalions among the Free Syrian Force there as well as Sunni, and I have talked to Alawite business community members who were supporting the effort there in Aleppo to hold on.

Ms. KABAWAT. Exactly. We need first to have a safe place for this community, once we stop the barrel bombs then support them with moderate oppositions in all the way we can and we get a good example in other local councils. And me, as a witness, they knew that I am Christian and I have been working with the civil society to empowering the local council and others.

And I know in Syria, what you see in sectarianism now it is a reaction because of all the death it happens. But in the end of the day with community we live together, the minute the death toll will stop the Syrian people can at least continue to live and they can live together.

Chairman ROYCE. Well, thank you. I want to thank all of our witnesses for their moving and insightful testimony here today. And ISIS is in fact conducting a war against religious minorities, against tolerance, and, as you have shared, against civilization. And I want to thank our panelists for bringing the voice of the persecuted, the voice of the Christians and the Yazidis and the moderate Muslims and many others to us here today.

And the committee has long been focused on ensuring a robust humanitarian response and an effective security strategy as well, but on the humanitarian response and the legislation that we have on the floor of the House, thank you for supporting that legislation today. And I think your appeals for safe zones and the longing to return to your homes have given us new facts to consider and now, I think, to consider with an indelible human face.

So Sister, thank you, and to all our panelists, thank you very much for being with us.

We stand adjourned.

[Whereupon, at 11:51 a.m., the committee was adjourned.]

APPENDIX

MATERIAL SUBMITTED FOR THE RECORD

FULL COMMITTEE HEARING NOTICE
COMMITTEE ON FOREIGN AFFAIRS
U.S. HOUSE OF REPRESENTATIVES
WASHINGTON, DC 20515-6128

Edward R. Royce (R-CA), Chairman

May 13, 2015

TO: MEMBERS OF THE COMMITTEE ON FOREIGN AFFAIRS

You are respectfully requested to attend an OPEN hearing of the Committee on Foreign Affairs, to be held in Room 2172 of the Rayburn House Office Building (and available live on the Committee website at http://www.ForeignAffairs.house.gov):

DATE: Wednesday, May 13, 2015

TIME: 10:00 a.m.

SUBJECT: Ancient Communities Under Attack: ISIS's War on Religious Minorities

WITNESSES: Sister Diana Momeka, OP
                   Dominican Sisters of Saint Catherine of Siena
                   Mosul, Iraq

                   Ms. Hind Kabawat
                   Director of Interfaith Peacebuilding
                   Center for World Religions, Diplomacy, and Conflict Resolution
                   George Mason University

                   Ms. Jacqueline Isaac
                   Vice President
                   Roads of Success

                   Katharyn Hanson, Ph.D.
                   Fellow
                   Penn Cultural Heritage Center
                   University of Pennsylvania Museum

By Direction of the Chairman

The Committee on Foreign Affairs seeks to make its facilities accessible to persons with disabilities. If you are in need of special accommodations, please call 202/225-5021 at least four business days in advance of the event, whenever practicable. Questions with regard to special accommodations in general (including availability of Committee materials in alternative formats and assistive listening devices) may be directed to the Committee.

49

COMMITTEE ON FOREIGN AFFAIRS
MINUTES OF FULL COMMITTEE HEARING

Day__*Wednesday*__Date_____*5/13/15*_____Room_____*2172*_____

Starting Time ____*10:06*____Ending Time ____*11:51*____

Recesses __*0*__ (____to____)(____to____)(____to____)(____to____)(____to____)(____to____)

Presiding Member(s)
Chairman Edward R. Royce

Check all of the following that apply:

Open Session ✓   Electronically Recorded (taped) ✓
Executive (closed) Session ☐   Stenographic Record ✓
Televised ✓

TITLE OF HEARING:

Ancient Communities Under Attack: ISIS' War on Religous Minorities

COMMITTEE MEMBERS PRESENT:

See attached.

NON-COMMITTEE MEMBERS PRESENT:

None

HEARING WITNESSES: Same as meeting notice attached? Yes ✓ No ☐
(If "no", please list below and include title, agency, department, or organization.)

STATEMENTS FOR THE RECORD: *(List any statements submitted for the record.)*

TIME SCHEDULED TO RECONVENE
or
TIME ADJOURNED *11:51*

Jean Marter, Director of Committee Operations

HOUSE COMMITTEE ON FOREIGN AFFAIRS

FULL COMMITTEE HEARING

PRESENT	MEMBER
X	Edward R. Royce, CA
X	Christopher H. Smith, NJ
X	Ileana Ros-Lehtinen, FL
X	Dana Rohrabacher, CA
X	Steve Chabot, OH
	Joe Wilson, SC
	Michael T. McCaul, TX
X	Ted Poe, TX
X	Matt Salmon, AZ
	Darrell Issa, CA
X	Tom Marino, PA
	Jeff Duncan, SC
X	Mo Brooks, AL
X	Paul Cook, CA
	Randy Weber, TX
X	Scott Perry, PA
X	Ron DeSantis, FL
X	Mark Meadows, NC
X	Ted Yoho, FL
	Curt Clawson, FL
X	Scott, DesJarlais, TN
	Reid Ribble, WI
	Dave Trott, MI
X	Lee Zeldin, NY
	Dan Donovan, NY

PRESENT	MEMBER
X	Eliot L. Engel, NY
X	Brad Sherman, CA
	Gregory W. Meeks, NY
X	Albio Sires, NJ
X	Gerald E. Connolly, VA
X	Theodore E. Deutch, FL
X	Brian Higgins, NY
	Karen Bass, CA
X	William Keating, MA
X	David Cicilline, RI
	Alan Grayson, FL
X	Ami Bera, CA
X	Alan S. Lowenthal, CA
	Grace Meng, NY
X	Lois Frankel, FL
X	Tulsi Gabbard, HI
X	Joaquin Castro, TX
X	Robin Kelly, IL
	Brendan Boyle, PA